DASH Diet Cookbook For Beginn

Discover the Low-Salt Recipes to Fuel Your Body and Delight Your Senses

TABLE OF CONTENTS

INTRODUCTION

Read this introduction if you're wondering how the Dash diet compares to other popular diets. We'll discuss what foods you can eat and which ones you should avoid or reduce. We'll also go over a few tips and tricks to make the diet as tasty and enjoyable as possible. And, we'll cover how to implement the diet into your daily routine to maximize your results. If you're still unsure whether the Dash diet is for you, check out our review of this popular diet.

Dash diet is a low-sodium diet that focuses on eating fresh, whole, plant-based foods. U.S.D.A. recommends DASH diet and stands for Dietary Approaches to Stop Hypertension or lowering blood pressure naturally through diet without side effects from medication (as compared to medicine). This diet is recommended for those who want to learn how to lose weight naturally and effectively.

1.1 How to Make the DASH Diet Work For You

Dash diet is excellent for your health because it encourages eating lots of whole-grain foods and fresh fruits and vegetables. It also excludes many processed foods high in sodium, sugar, and fat. In addition, this diet will help you lose weight naturally.

The DASH Diet has many benefits, but how do you make it work for you? The DASH Diet encourages you to eat five or more servings of fruits and vegetables every day. Examples of fruits and vegetables you can eat include bananas, raspberries, mango, and peaches. In addition, you can choose one medium apple or half a cup of frozen peaches for more fruit options. Alternatively, you can replace the meat in your meals with a vegetable or a fruit salad.

The DASH diet allows you to eat out, but you need to be cautious about the foods you choose. Most restaurant meals are fatty, salty, and oversized. To stay within the DASH diet, you should limit your intake of salt and condiments. You can still enjoy alcohol in moderation. If you are unsure how to make the foods you eat on the DASH diet, you can find recipes online.

The DASH diet also limits your sodium intake. High sodium diets can affect otherwise healthy people. You should avoid processed foods, packaged potato snacks, and white bread. You should also limit your intake of enriched grains like white bread and pasta. Frozen meals, convenience store snacks, and fast food are all foods with high sodium. Alcohol is another food group to limit. Not only does alcohol cause hypertension, but it can also damage your liver.

1.2 Dash diet vs other diets

There are pros and cons to the DASH diet. The DASH diet is unlikely to offer any significant benefits for healthy individuals. However, individuals with heart conditions or high blood pressure may benefit from a DASH-based diet. People on this diet should not use salt in their cooking but instead, add a few tablespoons of spices to their dishes. They should also limit the amount of salt in their beverages, as it increases the amount of sodium in their blood.

The DASH diet is also known for its focus on fruits and vegetables. The diet promotes eating various lean meats, whole grains, vegetables, and low-fat dairy foods. The DASH diet also encourages using many vegetable oils, including olive, canola, and margarine, instead of oily cooking oils. Those who follow the DASH diet should replace high-calorie salad dressings with low-fat alternatives.

One of the benefits of the DASH diet is its potential for lowering blood pressure without medication. Its low-sodium diet combined with increased intake of whole grains, vegetables and fruits, and lean protein reduces systolic blood pressure by 8-14 points. These reductions in blood pressure may also help lower risk of cardiovascular disease. In addition, DASH diet promotes an increased intake of fruits, vegetables, whole grains, fish, poultry, and nuts.

The DASH diet is not for everyone. For example, people suffering from high blood pressure may not be suitable for it. Also, it is not for everyone and requires a calorie-restricted diet. Diets with low-fat components may be the most suitable choice for some people. While it may be hard for some people to follow the DASH diet, it does have other benefits. It may even lower your risk of developing cancer.

The DASH diet requires significant changes in a person's diet and is hard to follow. It limits salt and fat intake significantly. It also requires significant cuts in precooked foods. As a result, many people have trouble following the DASH diet. And even if you do manage to stick to the diet, you are unlikely to see any results in the long run. You'll need to see your doctor regularly to check on the results of the DASH diet.

1.3 Tips and tricks of the diet for limiting sodium

To minimize sodium intake on the Dash Diet, check each food's nutritional content. For example, avoid poultry packed with a sodium solution when choosing your dinners. You can also try replacing the sodium in meat and poultry with herbs and citrus. Also, note down your serving size, and check the nutritional facts of each food. Finally, cook your food at a lower temperature to avoid excess sodium.

Aim to cook at home more often. Using fresh ingredients and cooking from scratch is a great way to limit sodium. Avoid going out to eat and try to cook at home more often. Taking a food log is helpful in monitoring sodium intake. It can take about a week to calculate your daily intake. To make it easier, try to cook dinner at least once a week. To cut down on eating out, use recipes that are low in sodium and avoid using salt shakers. Look for packaged food with a Nutrition Facts label. Choose foods with less than 2,300 milligrams of sodium per serving. When you are eating out, choose unsalted or no-salt-added products. Try to ensure fruits and vegetables cover at least half of plate. These foods are natural sources of fiber and are low in sodium. It also helps you lose weight, which is great for your overall health.

Another tip to limit sodium on the DASH Diet is to eat more fruits and vegetables. Eat more fruits and vegetables than you normally do, and you will be adding fiber and potassium to your diet. As you can see, eating more fruits and vegetables increases your blood potassium level and triggers the kidneys to eliminate extra sodium and fluid from the body. This helps lower blood pressure and reduces your risk of a heart attack.

1.4 Foods allowed and to avoid or reduce

A DASH diet aims to lower blood pressure by reducing sodium in the body. According to the National Institutes of Health, sodium intake should not exceed 2,300 milligrams per day. High blood pressure is the silent killer - most people don't experience symptoms for decades, and it often does not cause any other symptoms unless it becomes complicated. This diet also promotes weight loss. There are some foods you should avoid when eating the DASH diet, but don't worry, there are recipes available that are heart-healthy and delicious.

A good example of what you should limit on the DASH diet is red meat. The DASH diet encourages the consumption of fruits, whole grains, vegetables, lean meats, and low-fat dairy products. However, you should cut back on red meat because it is high in saturated fat and has been linked to coronary heart disease. Therefore, it's best to cut down on meat intake by a half or third at each meal.

1.5 Tacking weight loss

While many people associate the DASH diet with losing weight, that isn't the case. Instead of weight loss, this plan teaches you how to make healthier food choices for life. Written by Ashley Mateo, RRCA-certified running coach, the Dash diet isn't a crash diet. Instead, it's an exercise plan that focuses on heart-healthy foods from your local grocery store. These include whole grains, lean proteins, and low-fat dairy. The DASH diet is also free of sodium and saturated fat, which are common on other diets.

While many people think of this diet as low-fat and high-protein, this is not the case. Many people have high blood pressure and a heart condition, so the DASH diet focuses on reducing the risk of high blood pressure and lowering cholesterol. Using the Lose It! app to monitor your progress is a great tool to help you stick to your goals. Just make sure you follow the recommended serving sizes, and don't go overboard with the carbs. The DASH Diet focuses on whole, unrefined foods that are as close to their natural state as possible. It emphasizes lean proteins such as chicken, fish, and beef, as well as low-fat dairy products. You should also eat a lot of vegetables, which should comprise between four and five servings each day. One serving size equals half a cup of raw vegetables or one cup of cooked vegetables.

While the DASH diet does not require calorie counting, it does recommend a specific number of servings of specific foods. You can easily reach this target by adjusting your daily calorie goal. To maximize your weight loss efforts, the DASH diet encourages the eating of 6 servings of lean meat, poultry, and fish each day. The standard serving sizes

are 500-600kJ. The DASH Diet is ideal for those with a higher energy requirement, but this plan isn't for everyone.
While the DASH Diet was originally developed to treat hypertension, it has been found to be effective at boosting weight loss. Its goal is to reduce sodium, fats, and refined sugars, which are the main causes of hypertension. Currently, one in three adults in the US suffer from high blood pressure, and it's one of the leading causes of heart disease. In addition, the DASH Diet is less restrictive than other weight loss programs.

1.6 FAQs

Q. Should I count calories?
A. No. The DASH Diet is rich in whole food and low in saturated fat, so calorie counting isn't necessary.
Q. Will the DASH Diet make me constipated?
A. No. The high-fiber content ensures you'll be as regular as ever, while the low-sodium diet will reduce problems from excess sodium.
Q. Which fruits and vegetables are best for me?
A. All fresh produce is good for you and should be included in your diet. It's best to select the highest-quality foods you can afford.
Q. Can I have any "bad" foods on the DASH Diet?
A. No, although it may seem hard at first there are no "bad" foods as long as they are consumed in the right quantity and proportion to other food groups.
Q. Should I start with phase 1?
A. No. People who are healthy and eat a very healthy diet can go straight to phase 2 of the DASH Diet.
Q. Which phase should I pick?
A. The first phase is for beginners, so if you're healthy and have been eating a healthy diet for many years you can skip phase 1 and move straight to phase 2, but it's important that you try at least one meal of both phases to see which you feel best on.
Q. Is it possible to drink coffee?
A. Yes, as long as it is not added sugar or creamer.
Q. What about alcohol?
A. Alcohol has many health benefits and is fine to have up to one or two drinks a day, but going over this amount can be dangerous for your health, so don't go over the safe limits that are set for you in phase 2 of the DASH Diet.
Q. How long does it take to get used to the DASH Diet?
A. As long as you don't add more fat, sugar, or salt to your diet it will be very easy to adapt. Some people take only a few days to get used to the diet, while others take longer.
Q. Can I go on the DASH Diet if I have a history of heart disease?
A. Yes, as long as you follow all the recommendations of the DASH Diet in terms of healthy fats and low sodium.
Q. What about my sleep patterns?

A. I don't think it's important to determine how well you sleep every night, as long as you don't try to force yourself to get more than six hours a night, as this may be counter-productive if your body is telling you it needs more sleep than this.
Q. Should I exercise?
A. Yes, it's very important to exercise on a daily basis for at least thirty minutes if you can.
Q. How will the DASH Diet benefit me physically?
A. Studies have shown that the DASH Diet cuts down your risk of stroke and heart disease.
Q. How will the DASH Diet benefit me mentally?
A. The DASH Diet will reduce your risk of developing Alzheimer's and other mental disorders by cutting the risk of heart disease.
Q. How will the DASH Diet benefit me financially?
A. The "dash" diet will save you money as you won't need to buy any processed foods or other unhealthy extras that may come with them.

1 BREAKFAST

1.1 Millet Cream

Serves: 4 | Preparation Time: 10 minutes | Cooking Time: 30 minutes

Ingredients:

- low-fat milk - 14 oz.
- millet - 1 c.
- liquid honey - 1 tsp.
- vanilla extract - ½ tsp.

Procedure:

1. Using a medium high source of heat, set a pot in place. Add in the milk and let simmer. Mix in vanilla extract and millet and let cook for about 30 minutes as you stir constantly.
2. Apply a topping of honey to the ready millet cream.

Nutrition per serving:

989 calories, 5.9g protein, 37.9g carbs, 200mg sugars, 2.1g fat, 189mg sodium.

1.2 The Amazing Feta Hash

Serves: 6 | Preparation Time: 10 minutes | Cooking Time: 25 minutes

Ingredients:

- hash browns - 16 oz.
- low-fat feta, crumbled - 2 oz.
- olive oil - 1 tbsp.
- beaten eggs - 4
- soy milk - 1/3 c.
- chopped yellow onion - 1

Procedure:

1. Using a medium high source of heat, set a pan in place. Add in your oil and heat before mixing in hash browns. Allow to saute for approximately 5 mins.
2. Toss in the remaining ingredients with the exception of cheese. Let your mixture cook for an additional 5 minutes.
3. Add sprinkles of cheese to top. Set pan in your oven. Cook for 15 minutes at 390°F.

Nutrition per serving:

303 calories, 8.2g protein, 29.6g carbs, 17.1g fat, 2.87g fiber, 120mg cholesterol, 415mg sodium, 525mg potassium.

1.3 Sausage Casserole

Serves: 4 | Preparation Time: 10 minutes | Cooking Time: 35 minutes

Ingredients:

- beaten eggs - 2
- chopped onion - 1
- chopped chili pepper - 1
- olive oil - 1 tbsp.
- ground sausages - 1 c.

- chili flakes - 1 tsp.

Procedure:

1. Using a pan, mix in sausages, onion, and olive oil.
2. Mix in the remaining ingredients. Let your mixture roast for approximately 5 minutes before transferring to oven.
3. Place in the oven preheated to attain 370°F and allow to bake through for 25 minutes.

Nutrition per serving:

74 calories, 3.3g protein, 2.8 g carbs, 5.9g fat, 0.52g fiber, 84mg cholesterol, 35mg sodium, 75mg potassium.

1.4 Apples and Raisins Bowls

Serves: 4 | Preparation Time: 5 minutes | Cooking Time: 15 minutes

Ingredients:

- blackberries - 1 c.
- ground cardamom - 1 tsp.
- coconut milk - 1 ½ c.
- raisins - ¼ c.
- peeled, cored and cubed apples - 2
- coconut cream - 1 c.

Procedure:

1. Using a pot, pour in your coconut milk and let boil.
2. Stir in all the other ingredients.
3. Set heat to medium high and allow to simmer for 15 minutes.

Nutrition per serving:

266.1 calories, 2.61g protein, 14.4g carbs, 15.6g fat, 5.3g fiber, 0mg cholesterol, 65mg sodium, 374mg potassium

1.5 Dill Omelet

Serves: 6 | Preparation Time: 10 minutes | Cooking Time: 6 minutes

Ingredients:

- low-fat milk - 2 tbsps.
- white pepper - ¼ tsp.
- beaten eggs - 6
- chopped dill - 2 tbsps.
- avocado oil - 1 tbsp.

Procedure:

1. Using a skillet, heat avocado oil.
2. Using a bowl, mix the other ingredients.
3. Transfer the egg mixture to the hot oil. Allow your omelet to cook for 6 minutes.

Nutrition per serving:

71 calories, 6g protein, 1.4g carbs, 4.8g fat, 0.3g fiber, 164mg cholesterol, 66mg sodium, 109mg potassium.

1.6 Cheese Hash Browns

Serves: 6 | Preparation Time: 10 minutes | Cooking Time: 30 minutes

Ingredients:

- olive oil - 1 tsp.
- beaten eggs - 3
- hash browns - 2 c.
- shredded vegan mozzarella - 3 oz.

Procedure:

1. Set a pan in a pan. Add in olive oil and heat. Mix in your hash browns.
2. Allow 5 minutes of roasting as you occasionally stir.
3. Pour your eggs over the roasted hash browns. Set in your oven preheated at 380°F.
4. Allow the mixture to bake for 20 minutes. Enjoy.

Nutrition per serving:

212 calories, 4.9g protein, 21.8g carbs, 12.4g fat, 1.6g fiber, 83mg cholesterol, 316mg sodium, 328mg potassium.

1.7 Tomato and Spinach Eggs

Serves: 4 | Preparation Time: 10 minutes | Cooking Time: 20 minutes

Ingredients:

- low-fat milk - ½ c.
- whisked eggs - 8
- freshly chopped spinach - 1 c.
- chopped red onion - 1
- canola oil - 1 tbsp.
- cubed cherry tomatoes - 1 c.

Procedure:

1. Using a medium high source of heat, set a pan in place, add in oil and heat. Stir in onion and let cook for approx. 3 minutes.
2. Add in spinach and tomatoes. Stir well and let continue cooking for an additional 2 minutes.
3. Toss in eggs mixed with milk.
4. Transfer to a pan and place in your oven preheated at 390°F and cook for 15 more minutes.
5. Set in serving plates and enjoy.

Nutrition per serving:

202 calories, 15.4g protein, 7.2g carbs, 12.5g fat, 1.5g fiber, 332mg cholesterol, 218mg sodium, 354mg potassium

1.8 Scallions and Sesame Seeds Omelet

Serves: 4 | Preparation Time: 5 minutes | Cooking Time: 10 minutes

Ingredients:

- whisked eggs - 4
- olive oil - 1 tbsp.
- sesame seeds - 1 tsp.
- chopped scallions - 2
- chopped cilantro - 1 tbsp.

Procedure:

1. Place a pan over a medium high source of heat. Add in oil and

heat. Add in scallions and stir. Sauté for 2 minutes.

2. Mix in the remaining ingredients. Toss and spread the omelet to your pan. Cook until well done on one side for 3 minutes.
3. Flip and continue cooking the other side for 2 additional minutes.

Nutrition per serving:

101 calories, 5.9g protein, 1.4g carbs, 8.3g fat, 0.5g fiber, 164mg cholesterol, 63mg sodium, 97mg potassium

1.9 Omelet with Peppers

Serves: 4 | Preparation Time: 10 minutes | Cooking Time: 15 minutes

Ingredients:

- beaten eggs - 4
- margarine - 1 tbsp.
- chopped bell peppers - 1 c.
- chopped scallions - 2 oz.

Procedure:

1. Using a skillet, toss in margarine and heat well until melted.
2. Using a mixing bowl, add scallions, eggs, bell peppers and mix well.
3. Set your egg mixture in your hot skillet and allow the omelet to roast for about 12 minutes.

Nutrition per serving:

102 calories, 6.1g protein, 3.7g carbs, 7.3g fat, 0.8g fiber, 164mg cholesterol, 98mg sodium, 156mg potassium.

1.10 Artichoke Eggs

Serves: 4 | Preparation Time: 5 minutes | Cooking Time: 20 minutes

Ingredients:

- beaten eggs - 5
- chopped low-fat feta - 2 oz.
- chopped yellow onion - 1
- canola oil - 1 tbsp.
- chopped cilantro - 1 tbsp.
- chopped artichoke hearts, canned - 1 c.

Procedure:

1. Using the oil, grease 4 ramekins.
2. Mix all the remaining ingredients and divide the mix between the prepared ramekins.
3. Preheat you oven to 380F and allow to bake for approximately 20 minutes.

Nutrition per serving:

176 calories, 10 protein, 7.6g carbs, 12g fat, 2.7g fiber, 219mg cholesterol, 256mg sodium, 238mg potassium.

1.11 Bean Casserole

Serves: 8 | Preparation Time: 10 minutes | Cooking Time: 30 minutes

Ingredients:

- chopped white onions - ½ c.
- beaten eggs - 5
- chopped bell pepper - ½ c.
- red kidney beans (cooked) - 1 c.
- low-fat shredded mozzarella cheese - 1 c.

Procedure:

1. Using a casserole mold, spread the kidney beans and add in bell pepper and onions.
2. Mix cheese and eggs and transfer to the beans mixture.
3. Allow to bake at a heat of 380°F for about 30 minutes.

Nutrition per serving:

143 calories, 12.6g protein, 17g carbs, 3.2g fat, 4.5g fiber, 107mg cholesterol, 163mg sodium, 376mg potassium.

1.12 Strawberry Sandwich

Serves: 4 | Preparation Time: 5 minutes | Cooking Time: 0 minutes

Ingredients:

- low-fat yogurt - 4 tbsps.
- sliced strawberries - 4
- whole-wheat bread slices - 4

Procedure:

1. Spread the bread with yogurt and then top with sliced strawberries.

Nutrition per serving:

84 calories, 4.6g protein, 13.6g carbs, 1.2g fat, 2.1g fiber, 1mg cholesterol, 143mg sodium, 124mg potassium.

2 SALADS

2.1 Shrimp and Veggie Salad

Serves: 4 | Preparation Time: 10 minutes | Cooking Time: 0 minutes

Ingredients:

- halved cherry tomatoes - 2 c.
- Cracked black pepper - 1
- freshly trimmed asparagus spears - 12 oz.
- cooked frozen and peeled shrimp - 16 oz.
- Cracker bread - 1
- watercress - 4 c.
- bottled light raspberry - ½ c.

Procedure:

1. Using a large skillet, add asparagus in some boiled lightly salted water. Allow to cook for approximately 3 minutes while covered. Drain using a colander. Use cold running water to cool.
2. Set the asparagus in 4 dinner plates; add a topping of cherry tomatoes, shrimp and watercress. Drizzle over with raspberry.
3. Add sprinkles of cracked black pepper and enjoy alongside cracker bread.

Nutrition per serving:

Calories 155.5, Fat 1.4 g, Carbs 15 g, Protein 22 g, Sodium: 346 mg, Potassium: 714mg

2.2 Salmon and Spinach Salad

Serves: 4 | Preparation Time: 10 minutes | Cooking Time: 0 minutes

Ingredients:

- drained and flaked canned salmon - 1 c.
- grated lime zest - 1 tbsp.
- lime juice - 1 tbsp.
- fat-free yogurt - 3 tbsps.
- baby spinach - 1 c.
- drained and chopped capers - 1 tsp.
- chopped red onion - 1
- pepper – ¼ tsp.

Procedure:

1. Using a bowl, add salmon, zest, lime juice and other ingredients
2. Toss well and serve

Nutrition per serving:

Calories 155.5| Fat 1.4 g| Carbs 15 g| Protein 22 g | Sodium: 366mg| Potassium: 544mg

2.3 Corn Salad

Serves: 6 | Preparation Time: 10 minutes | Cooking Time: 2 hours |

Ingredients:

- prosciutto, sliced into strips - 2 oz.
- olive oil - 1 tsp.
- corn - 2 c.
- salt-free tomato sauce - 1/2 c.
- minced garlic - 1 tsp.
- chopped green bell pepper - 1

Procedure:

1. Using a Slow Cooker, add oil to grease.
2. Add corn, tomato sauce, garlic, prosciutto, bell pepper to the Slow Cooker as you stir.
3. Set the lid in place and cook for 2 hour on HIGH setting.

Nutrition per serving:

Calories 158.5, Fat 1.4 g, Carbs 15 g, Protein 23 g, Sodium 332mg, Potassium 501mg

2.4 Watercress Salad

Serves: 4 | Preparation Time: 5 minutes | Cooking Time: 4 minutes

Ingredients:

- chopped asparagus - 2 c.
- cooked shrimp - 16 oz.
- torn watercress - 4 c.
- apple cider vinegar - 1 tbsp.
- olive oil - ¼ c.

Procedure:

1. In the mixing bowl mix up asparagus, shrimps, watercress, and olive oil.

Nutrition per serving:

264 calories | 28.3g protein | 4.5g carbs | 14.8g fat | 1.8g fiber | 239mg cholesterol | 300mg sodium | 393mg potassium.

2.5 Tuna Salad

Serves: 4 | Preparation: 15minutes | Cooking: 0 minutes

Ingredients:

- low-fat Greek yogurt - ½ c.
- canned tuna - 8 oz.
- freshly chopped parsley - ½ c.
- cooked corn kernels - 1 c.
- ground black pepper - ½ tsp.

Procedure:

1. Combine kernels, tuna, black pepper, and parsley.
2. Mix in yogurt and ensure you stir properly to get a homogenous salad.

Nutrition per serving:

173 calories, 17.7g protein, 13.7g carbs, 5.6g fat, 1.3g fiber, 19.3mg cholesterol, 57mg sodium, 393mg potassium.

2.6 Watermelon Salad

Serves: 6 | Preparation Time: 18 minutes | Cooking Time: 0 minutes

Ingredients:

- sea salt - ¼ tsp.
- black pepper - ¼ tsp.
- balsamic vinegar - 1 tbsp.
- quartered & seeded cantaloupe - 1
- small & seedless watermelon - 12
- fresh mozzarella balls, - 2 c.
- fresh and torn basil - 1/3 c.
- olive oil - 2 tbsps.

Procedure:

1. Scoop out balls of cantaloupe and put them in a colander over a bowl.
2. With a melon baller, slice the watermelon.
3. Allow your fruit to drain for ten minutes, and then refrigerate the juice.
4. Wipe the bowl dry, and then place your fruit in it.
5. Stir in basil, oil, vinegar, mozzarella and tomatoes before seasoning.
6. Mix well and enjoy.

Nutrition per serving:

Calories: 218, Protein: 10g, Fat: 13g, Sodium: 59mg, Potassium: 43mg.

2.7 Orange Celery Salad

Serves: 6 | Preparation Time: 16 minutes | Cooking Time: 0 minutes

Ingredients:

- fresh lemon juice - 1 tbsp.
- olive brine - 1 tbsp.
- olive oil - 1 tbsp.
- sliced red onion - ¼ c.
- fine sea salt - ¼ tsp.
- green olives - ½ c.
- peeled & sliced oranges - 2
- black pepper - ¼ tsp.
- celery stalks, sliced diagonally in ½ inch slices - 3

Procedure:

1. Using a shallow bowl, add in oranges, onion, olives, and celery.
2. Stir together oil, lemon juice & olive brine, pour this over your salad.
3. Add pepper and salt for seasoning and enjoy

Nutrition per serving:

Calories: 65, Protein: 2g, Fat: 0.2g, Sodium: 43mg, Potassium: 123mg.

2.8 Lettuce & Cucumber Salad

Serves: 4 | Preparation Time: 20 minutes| Cooking Time: 0 minutes

Ingredients:

- chopped romaine lettuce - 2 c.
- cooked corn kernels - 1 c.
- canola oil - 1 tbsp.
- cooked green beans, chopped roughly - ½ pound
- chopped cucumber - 1 c.

Procedure:

1. Using a salad bowl, add in the above ingredients and mix. Set in serving plates and serve

Nutrition per serving:

88 calories, 2.7g protein, 13.2g carbs, 4.2g fat, 3.4g fiber, 0mg cholesterol, 12mg sodium, 302mg potassium.

2.9 Seafood Arugula Salad

Serves: 4 | Preparation Time: 15 minutes | Cooking Time: 0 minutes

Ingredients:

- olive oil - 1 tbsp.
- cooked shrimps - 2 c.
- chopped cilantro - 1 tbsp.

Procedure:

1. Using a salad bowl, mix in all the above ingredients. Shake well to have a well combined mixture.

Nutrition per serving:

62 calories, 6.7g protein, 0.3g carbs, 3.8g fat, 0.2g fiber, 124mg cholesterol, 217mg sodium, 21mg potassium.

3 SOUPS

3.1 Lemon & Garlic Soup

Serves: 3 | Preparation Time: 10 minutes | Cooking Time: 0 minutes

Ingredients:

- chopped and pitted avocado - 1
- chopped cucumber - 1
- coconut aminos - ½ c.
- bunches spinach - 2
- chopped watermelon - 1 ½ c.
- chopped cilantro - 1 bunch
- Juice of 2 lemons
- lime juice - ½ c.

Procedure:

1. In a blender, add in avocado and cucumber and pulse carefully.
2. Add in spinach, cilantro, and watermelon. Blend well.
3. Mix in coconut aminos, lime juice and lemon juice and pulse again.
4. Set in soup bowls and enjoy.

Nutrition per serving:

Calories: 101, Fat: 7.3g, Carbs: 6.2g, Protein: 3.1g, Sodium: 228mg, Potassium: 1946 mg

3.2 Healthy Cucumber Soup

Serves: 4 | Preparation Time: 14 minutes| Cooking Time: 0 minutes

Ingredients:

- minced garlic - 2 tbsps.
- peeled and diced English cucumbers - 4 c.
- diced onions - ½ c.
- lemon juice - 1 tbsp.
- vegetable broth - 1 ½ c.
- sunflower seeds - ½ tsp.
- red pepper flakes - ¼ tsp.
- diced parsley - ¼ c.
- plain Greek yogurt - ½ c.

Procedure:

1. Add the listed ingredients to a blender and blend to emulsify (keep aside ½ cup of chopped cucumbers).
2. Blend until smooth.
3. Divide the soup amongst 4 servings and top with extra cucumbers.
4. Enjoy chilled!

Nutrition per serving:

Calories: 371, Fat: 36g, Carbs: 8g, Protein: 4g, Sodium: 240 mg, Potassium: 458 mg

3.3 Amazing Pumpkin Soup

Serves: 4 | Preparation Time: 5 minutes | Cooking Time: 25 minutes

Ingredients:

- halved, deseeded, peeled & cubed pumpkin - 1
- coconut milk - 1 c.
- chicken broth - 2 c.
- Pepper & thyme - ¼ tsp. each
- roasted seeds - ¼ c.

Procedure:

1. Using a crockpot, add in all the above ingredients except roasted seeds and set the lid in place.
2. Allow to cook on low for 25 minutes.
3. Set in a blender. Process well to obtain a smooth puree.
4. Add roasted seeds to garnish. Enjoy

Nutrition per serving:

Calories: 61, Fat: 2.2g, Net Carbs: 10.3g, Protein: 3.2g, Sodium: 254mg, Potassium: 505mg

3.4 Coconut Avocado Soup

Serves: 4 | Preparation Time: 5 minutes | Cooking Time: 5-10 minutes

Ingredients:

- vegetable stock - 2 c.
- Thai green curry paste - 2 tsps.
- Pepper – ¼ tsp.
- chopped avocado - 1
- chopped cilantro - 1 tbsp.
- Lime wedges
- coconut milk - 1 c.

Procedure:

1. Add milk, curry paste, avocado, pepper to blender and blend.
2. Set a pan over a medium high source of heat.
3. Place the mixture on your pan and heat before simmering for 5 minutes.
4. Stir in seasoning, cilantro and simmer for 1 minute.
5. Enjoy!

Nutrition per serving:

Calories: 250, Fat: 30g, Net Carbs: 2g, Protein: 4g, Sodium: 42mg, Potassium: 487mg

3.5 Pumpkin & Garlic Soup

Serves: 4 | Preparation Time: 10 minutes | Cooking Time: 6 hours

Ingredients:

- pumpkin chunks - 1 pound
- diced onion - 1
- vegetable stock - 2 c.
- crushed garlic - 1 tsp.
- coconut cream - 1 2/3 c.
- almond butter - ½ stick
- crushed ginger - 1 tsp.
- Pepper - ¼ tsp.

Procedure:

1. In a slow cooker, add all ingredients. Mix well and cook for 6 hours on HIGH setting.
2. Transfer the mixture to your immersion blender and puree your soup. Enjoy!

Nutrition per serving:

Calories: 234, Fat: 20g, Carbs: 11.2g, Protein: 2.1g, Sodium: 326mg, Potassium: 1321mgCelery, Cucumber and Zucchini Soup
Serves: 2 | Preparation Time: 10minutes | Cooking Time: 0 minutes

Ingredients:

- chopped celery stalks - 3
- cubed cucumber - 7 oz.
- olive oil - 1 tbsp.
- fresh 30% low fat cream - 2/5 c.
- chopped red bell pepper - 1
- chopped dill - 1 tbsp.
- cubed zucchini - 10 ½ oz.
- Sunflower seeds and pepper, to taste

Procedure:

1. Put the vegetables in a juicer and juice well.
2. Add in fresh cream and olive oil. Mix well.
3. Add pepper and sauce for seasoning.
4. Garnish with dill.
5. Enjoy while chilled.

Nutrition per serving:

Calories: 325, Fat: 32g, Carbs: 10g, Protein: 4g, Sodium: 477mg, Potassium: 1138mg

3.6 Vegetable Barley & Turkey Soup

Serves: 3 | Preparation Time: 10 minutes | Cooking Time: 23 minutes

Ingredients:

- canola oil - 1 tbsp.
- carrots - 5
- onion - 1
- quick-cooking barley - 2/3 c.
- reduced-sodium chicken broth - 6 c.
- cooked & cubed turkey breast - 2 c.
- fresh baby spinach - 2 c.
- pepper - ½ tsp.

Procedure:

1. Using an expansive pot set over a medium high source of heat, add oil and heat.
2. Add in your onion and carrots. Mix well before cooking for 5 minutes to ensure the carrots become delicate.
3. Add in broth and barley and allow to boil. Reduce the heat and let

simmer for 15 minutes to make the grains delicate.

4. Add in pepper, spinach, and turkey. Combine well and heat for 3 minutes until well done.

Nutrition per serving:

Calories 209, Fat 5g, Carbs 24g, Sugars 4.3g, Protein 2.4g, Sodium 937mg, Potassium 2397mg

3.7 Tomato Green Bean Soup

Serves: 4 | Preparation: 10 minutes | Cooking: 35 minutes

Ingredients:

- chopped onion - 1 c.
- chopped carrots - 1 c.
- butter - 2 tsps.
- reduced-sodium chicken broth - 6 c.
- fresh green beans - 1 pound
- garlic clove - 1
- diced fresh tomatoes - 3 c.
- minced fresh basil - ¼ c.
- salt - ½ tsp.
- pepper - ¼ tsp.

Procedure:

1. Using a vast pot, add in carrots and onion and sauté in a spread for 5 minutes.
2. Blend in the broth, beans, and garlic; heat to the point of boiling.
3. Decrease heat; spread and stew for 20 minutes or until vegetables are delicate.
4. Blend in the tomatoes, basil, salt, and pepper. Spread and stew 5 minutes longer.

Nutrition per serving:

Calories 58, Fat 1g, Carbs 10g, Sugars 5g, Protein 4g, Sodium 203mg, Potassium 832mg

3.8 Mushroom Barley Soup

Serves: 4 | Preparation Time: 15minutes | Cooking Time: 45 minutes

Ingredients:

- canola oil - 1 tbsp.
- onions - 1½ c.
- carrots - ¾ c.
- dried thyme - 1 tsp.
- black pepper - 1/8 tsp.
- garlic - ½ tsp.
- vegetable stock - 8 c.
- sliced mushrooms - 1 c.
- pearl barley - ¾ c.
- dry sherry - 3 oz.
- potato - ½
- chopped green onions - ¼ c.

Procedure:

1. Using a stock pot, add in oil and heat. Mix in onions, carrots, pepper, thyme, mushrooms, and garlic. Saute the mixture until onion is translucent for 5 minutes.
2. Mix in veggie stock and barley. Allow the mixture to heat until it boils.
3. Reduce heat and let simmer for approximately 20 minutes until barley becomes tender.
4. Mix in potato and sherry and continue simmering until potato becomes well-cooked for about 15 minutes.
5. Add green onions to garnish.
6. Enjoy

Nutrition per serving:

Calories 129, Fat 5.6g, Carbs 18.2g, Sugars 2.2g, Protein 3.3g, Sodium 22mg, Potassium 562mg

4 FISH AND SHELLFISH

4.1 Cilantro Halibut

Serves: 4 | Preparation time: 10 minutes | Cooking time: 15 minutes

Ingredients:

- chopped shallots - 2
- olive oil - 1 tbsp.
- boneless halibut fillets - 4
- chopped cilantro - 1 tbsp.
- lemon juice - 2 tsps.

Procedure:

1. Apply oil to a pan for greasing. Set your fish inside before topping with cilantro, lemon juice and shallot.
2. Set in oven preheated at 365°F. Bake until done for 15 minutes.

Nutrition per serving:

365calories, 61.3g protein, 3.6g carbs, 10.4g fat, 1g fiber, 93g cholesterol, 171mg sodium, 1502mg potassium

4.2 Shallot and Salmon Mix

Serves: 4 | Preparation time: 10 minutes | Cooking time: 15 minutes

Ingredients:

- olive oil - 2 tbsps.
- boneless salmon fillets - 4
- chopped shallot - 1
- water - ½ c.
- chopped parsley - 2 tbsps.

Procedure:

1. Set a pan over a medium high source of heat. Add oil and heat.

Mix in shallot and allow to sauté for 4 minutes.

2. Mix in water, parsley and salmon.
3. Set the lid in place and allow to cook for 11 minutes while heat is set to medium.

Nutrition per serving:

369calories, 37.3g protein, 3.6g carbs, 24g fat, 1.7g fiber, 78g cholesterol, 97mg sodium, 806mg potassium

4.3 Limes and Shrimps Skewers

Serves: 4 | Preparation Time: 15 minutes | Cooking Time: 6 minutes

Ingredients:

- peeled shrimps - 1 pound
- lime - 1
- lemon juice - 1 tsp.
- white pepper - ½ tsp.

Procedure:

1. Cut the lime into wedges.
2. Then sprinkle the shrimps with lemon juice and white pepper.
3. String the lime and lime wedges in the wooden skewers one-by-one.
4. Preheat the grill to 400F.
5. Put the shrimp skewers in grill. Cook each side for 3 minutes until the shrimps become light pink.

Nutrition per serving:

141 calories | 26g protein | 3.7g carbs | 2g fat | 0.6g fiber | 239mg cholesterol | 277mg sodium | 214mg potassium.

4.4 Tuna and Pineapple Kebob

Serves: 4 | Preparation Time: 10 minutes | Cooking Time: 8 minutes

Ingredients:

- tuna fillet - 12 oz.
- peeled pineapple - 8 oz.
- olive oil - 1 tsp.
- ground fennel - ¼ tsp.

Procedure:

1. Chop the tuna and pineapple on medium size cubes. Sprinkle ground fennel and olive oil over the mixture.
2. String them in the skewers and place them in preheated oven to 400F grill.
3. Cook the kebobs for 4 minutes per side.

Nutrition per serving:

347 calories, 18.2g protein, 7.5g carbs, 27.6g fat, 0.8g fiber, 0mg cholesterol, 1mg sodium, 64mg potassium.

4.5 Coconut Cod

Serves: 4 | Preparation Time: 10 minutes | Cooking Time: 25 minutes

Ingredients:

- coconut shred - 2 tbsps.

- boneless cod fillets - 4
- chopped red onion - 1
- olive oil - 2 tbsps.
- coconut milk - ¼ c.

Procedure:

1. Set a pan over a medium high source of heat. Add in oil and heat. Mix in onion and let cook for 5 minutes.
2. Mix in fish plus the other ingredients. Cook for an additional 20 minutes.

Nutrition per serving:

207calories, 23.5g protein, 11.6g carbs, 8.4g fat, 3.5g fiber, 40g cholesterol, 135mg sodium, 399mg potassium

4.6 Ginger Sea Bass

Serves: 4 | Preparation Time: 10 minutes | Cooking Time: 20 minutes

Ingredients:

- grated ginger - 1 tbsp.
- olive oil - 2 tbsps.
- boneless sea bass fillets - 4

Procedure:

1. Rub the sea bass fillet with ginger and sprinkle with olive oil.
2. Set the fish in a tray. Preheat oven to 365F. Bake for about 20 minutes.

Nutrition per serving:

191calories, 24g protein, 1g carbs, 9.7g fat, 0.2g fiber, 54g cholesterol, 89mg sodium, 353mg potassium

4.7 Baked Cod

Serves: 2 | Preparation Time: 10 min | Cooking Time: 20 minutes

Ingredients:

- cod fillet - 10 oz.
- Italian seasonings - 1 tsp.
- margarine - 1 tbsp.

Procedure:

1. Rub the baking pan with margarine.
2. Then chop the cod and sprinkle with Italian seasonings.
3. Set the fish in baking pan and use a foil to cover.
4. Bake the meal at 375F for 20 minutes.

Nutrition per serving:

170 calories, 25.1g protein, 0.3g carbs, 7.6g fat, 0g fiber, 70mg cholesterol, 155mg sodium, 4mg potassium.

4.8 Five-Spices Sole

Serves: 3 | Preparation Time: 10 minutes| Cooking Time: 11 minutes

Ingredients:

- sole fillets - 3
- five-spice seasonings - 1 tbsp.

- coconut oil - 1 tbsp.

Procedure:

1. Rub the sole fillets with seasonings.
2. Using a skillet, add in coconut oil and heat for 2 minutes.
3. Place sole fillets in hot oil and cook each side for 4.5 minutes.

Nutrition per serving:

204 calories, 31.8g protein, 1g carbs, 6.5g fat, 2.2g fiber, 86mg cholesterol, 133mg sodium, 437mg potassium.

4.9 Parsley Shrimp

Serves: 4 | Preparation Time: 10 minutes | Cooking Time: 10 minutes

Ingredients:

- peeled and deveined shrimp - 1 pound
- Juice of 1 lemon
- olive oil - 1 tbsp.
- chopped parsley - a bunch

Procedure:

1. Using a pan set over a medium high source of heat, add oil and allow to heat. Mix in shrimp and let each side cook for 3 minutes.
2. Mix in parsley and lemon juice before cooking for 4 more minutes.

Nutrition per serving:

190calories, 26.2g protein, 8.3g carbs, 5.5g fat, 0.7g fiber, 239g cholesterol, 279mg sodium, 267mg potassium

4.10 Tender Salmon with Chives

Serves: 4 | Preparation Time: 10 minutes | Cooking Time: 20 minutes

Ingredients:

- chopped yellow onion - 1
- chili powder - 1 tsp.
- olive oil - 2 tbsps.
- water - ¼ c.
- skinless and boneless salmon fillets - 4
- chopped chives - 2 tbsps.

Procedure:

1. Set a pan over a medium source of heat. Add oil and heat. Mix in onion and sauté for 3 minutes.
2. Set in salmon and allow each side to cook for 5 minutes.
3. Mix in chili powder, chives and water before cooking for 12 more minutes.

Nutrition per serving:

317calories, 35.1g protein, 3.7g carbs, 18.7g fat, 1.1g fiber, 78g cholesterol, 169mg sodium, 749mg potassium

4.11 Fennel and Salmon

Serves: 4 | Preparation Time: 5 minutes | Cooking Time: 15 minutes

Ingredients:

- skinless and boneless salmon fillets - 4
- chopped fennel bulb - 1
- water - ½ c.
- olive oil - 2 tbsps.
- lemon juice - 1 tbsp.
- chopped cilantro - 1 tbsp.

Procedure:

1. Set a pan over a medium high source of heat. Add in oil and heat. Mix in fennel before cooking for about 3 minutes.
2. Set in the fish. Cook each side for until browned 4 minutes.
3. Mix in remaining ingredients and allow to cook for an extra 8 minutes.

Nutrition per serving:

317calories, 35.4g protein, 4.9g carbs, 18.1g fat, 2g fiber, 78g cholesterol, 127mg sodium, 948mg potassium

4.12 Cod and Asparagus

Serves: 4 | Preparation Time: 10 minutes | Cooking Time: 25 minutes

Ingredients:

- olive oil - 1 tbsp.
- chopped red onion - 1
- boneless cod fillets - 1 pound
- trimmed asparagus - 1 bunch

Procedure:

1. Place the cod in the tray and sprinkle it with olive oil and red onion.
2. Add asparagus.
3. Bake the fish for 25 minutes at 365F.

Nutrition per serving:

298calories, 27.4g protein, 7.2g carbs, 19.1g fat, 2.6g fiber, 50g cholesterol, 111mg sodium, 268mg potassium

5 VEGETARIAN PLATES

5.1 Roasted Brussels Sprouts

Serves: 4 | Preparation Time: 5 minutes | Cooking Time: 35minutes

Ingredients:

- halved trimmed Brussels sprouts - 1½ pounds
- olive oil - 2 tbsps.
- salt - ¼ tsp.
- freshly ground black pepper - ½ tsp.

Procedure:

1. Preheat your oven to attain 400°F. Using a mixing bowl, mix in Brussels sprouts and olive oil. Toss well to evenly coat.
2. Set Brussels sprouts to a large baking sheet. Flip them over, so the cut-side faces down with the flat part touching the baking sheet. Sprinkle pepper and salt to the mixture.
3. Bake within 30 minutes to ensure the Brussels sprouts become crispy and lightly charred to the outside while toasted to the bottom side. Serve.

Nutrition per serving:

Calories: 134, Fat: 8g, Sodium: 189mg, Carbs: 15g, Protein: 6g, Potassium: 662mg

5.2 Chunky Black-Bean Dip

Serves: 2 | Preparation Time: 5 minutes | Cooking Time: 1 minutes

Ingredients:

- drained black beans, with liquid reserved - 1 (15 oz.) can
- chipotle peppers in adobo sauce - ½ can
- plain Greek yogurt - ¼ c.
- ground black pepper - ¼ tsp.

Procedure:

1. Using a blender, add in chipotle peppers, yogurt and beans. Mix well before processing to obtain a smooth consistency. Mix in part of reserved bean liquid (a tablespoon at a moment) to obtain a thinner consistency.
2. Add black pepper for seasoning and enjoy.

Nutrition per serving:

Calories: 70g, Fat: 1g, Sodium: 159mg, Carbs: 11g, Protein: 5g, Potassium: 281mg

5.3 Greek Flatbread with Spinach, Tomatoes & Feta

Serves: 2 | Preparation Time: 15 minutes | Cooking Time: 9 minutes

Ingredients:

- fresh and coarsely chopped baby spinach - 2 c.
- olive oil - 2 tsps.
- naan or flatbread - 2 slices
- sliced black olives - ¼ c.
- sliced plum tomatoes - 2
- Italian seasoning blend (salt-free) - ½ tsp.
- crumbled feta - ¼ c.

Procedure:

1. Preheat oven to attain 400°F. Using a skillet set in place over the medium high heat, add in 3 tbsps. water and heat. Mix in spinach, and steam for 2 minutes to wilt while covered. Drain any water in excess before placing aside.
2. Drizzle flatbreads with oil. To each of the flatbread, add olives, seasoning, spinach, feta and tomatoes to top. Bake until browned for 7 minutes. Slice in 4 pieces and enjoy.

Nutrition per serving:

Calories: 410, Fat: 16g, Carbs: 53g, Fiber: 7g, Protein: 16g , Sodium: 622mg, Potassium: 521mg

5.4 Black-Bean and Vegetable Burrito

Serves: 4 | Preparation Time: 15 minutes | Cooking Time: 15 minutes

Ingredients:

- olive oil - ½ tbsp.
- chopped red or green bell peppers - 2
- diced zucchini or summer squash - 1
- chili powder - ½ tsp.
- cumin - 1 tsp.
- ground black pepper – ¼ tsp.
- drained and rinsed black beans - 2 (14 oz.) cans
- halved cherry tomatoes - 1 c.
- whole-wheat tortillas - 4 (8-inch)
- Optional for **Serving:** spinach, chopped scallions, sliced avocado, or hot sauce

Procedure:

1. Set a saute pan on a medium high source of heat. Add in oil and heat. Mix in bell peppers and saute for 4 minutes until crisp and tender. Add the zucchini, chili powder, cumin, and black pepper, and continue to sauté for 5 minutes until vegetables become tender.
2. Add the black beans and cherry tomatoes and cook within 5 minutes. Divide between 4 burritos and serve topped with optional ingredients as desired. Enjoy immediately.

Nutrition per serving:

Calories: 311, Fat: 6g, Sodium: 199mg, Carbs: 52g, Protein: 19g, Potassium: 329mg

5.5 Red Beans and Rice

Serves: 2 | Preparation Time: 5 minutes | Cooking Time: 30 minutes

Ingredients:

- dry brown rice - ½ c.
- water, - 1 c. plus extra ¼ c.
- drained red beans - 1 (14 oz.) can
- ground cumin - 1 tbsp.
- Juice of 1 lime
- fresh spinach - 4 handfuls
- Optional toppings: Greek yogurt, avocado, chopped tomatoes, onions

Procedure:

1. Using a pot, mix rice plus water and let boil. Cover and lower your heat to a low simmer. Cook within 20 to 25 minutes or as per the directions on the package.
2. Meanwhile, add the beans, ¼ c. water, lime juice, and cumin to a medium skillet. Simmer within 5 to 7 minutes.
3. Once the liquid is reduced considerably, remove from the heat. Mix in spinach and allow to wilt for 3 minutes while covered. Add in beans and mix well. Enjoy alongside rice with toppings of your choice.

Nutrition per serving:

Calories: 232, Fat: 2g , Sodium: 210mg, Carbs: 41g , Protein: 13g, Potassium: 367mg

5.6 Veggie Pita Rolls

Serves: 2 | Preparation Time: 30 minutes| Cooking Time: 0 minutes

Ingredients:

- shredded romaine lettuce - 1 c.
- chopped cucumber - ½ c.
- chopped red onion - 1
- olive oil - 1 tbsp.
- black pepper – ¼ tsp.
- prepared hummus - ¼ c.
- chopped and seeded bell pepper - 1
- chopped and seeded tomato - 1
- finely minced garlic clove - 1
- fresh lime juice - ½ tbsp.
- warmed whole-wheat pita breads - 2

Procedure:

1. Using a bowl, mix in the above ingredients with exception of pitas and hummus. Toss gently and ensure they are well coated. Place

each pita bread onto serving plates.

2. Spread 2 tbsp. of hummus over a pita bread evenly. Top with salad and roll the pita bread.
3. Repeat with remaining pita bread, hummus and salad.

Nutrition per serving:

Calories: 334, Fat: 12g, Carbs: 51.6g, Fiber: 9g, Sugar: 6.9g, Protein: 10.5g, Sodium: 400mg, Potassium: 587mg

5.7 Veggies Stuffed Bell Peppers

Serves: 4 | Preparation Time: 15 minutes | Cooking Time: 25 minutes

Ingredients:

- fresh shiitake mushrooms - ½ lb.
- peeled garlic cloves - 2
- olive oil - 2 tbsps.
- black pepper – ¼ tsp.
- celery stalk - 1 c.
- unsalted walnuts - ½ c.
- Pinch of salt
- halved and deseeded bell peppers - 4

Procedure:

1. Preheat oven to attain 400 °F. Grease your baking sheet.
2. Using a food processor, mix in oil, salt, mushrooms, celery, garlic, walnuts, pepper and pulse to finely chop. Stuff bell peppers with the mushroom mixture.
3. Set them onto the prepared baking sheet. Bake until slightly brown for about 25 minutes. Enjoy while warm.

Nutrition per serving:

Calories: 213, Fat: 16.7g, Carbs: 13.7g, Fiber: 3.7g, Sugar: 7g, Protein: 7g , Sodium: 160mg, Potassium: 456mg

5.8 Rosemary Endives

Serves: 4 | Preparation Time: 10 minutes | Cooking Time: 20 Minutes

Ingredients:

- olive oil - 2 tbsps.
- dried rosemary - 1 tsp.
- halved endives - 2
- black pepper - ¼ tsp.
- turmeric powder - ½ tsp.

Procedure:

1. Using a baking pan, mix all ingredients as you toss for maximum coating. Set in your preheated oven to attain 400 °F and let bake well for 20 minutes.
2. Enjoy.

Nutrition per serving:

Calories: 66, Fat:7.1 g, Carbs:1.2 g, Protein:0.3 g, Sugars:1.3 g, Sodium:113 mg, Potassium: 411mg

5.9 Easy Chickpea Veggie Burgers

Serves: 4 | Preparation Time: 10 minutes | Cooking Time: 20 minutes

Ingredients:

- drained and rinsed chickpeas - 1 (15 oz) can
- onion powder - 1 tsp.
- thawed and frozen spinach - ½ c.
- rolled oats - ⅓ c.
- garlic powder - 1 tsp.

Procedure:

1. Set your oven to preheat to attain 400°F. Set a parchment paper to your baking sheet.
2. Using a mixing bowl, add half of the beans and mash until fairly smooth.
3. In a blender, add the remaining beans, spinach, oats, and spices. Blend until puréed. Add mixture to the bowl of mashed beans and stir until well combined.
4. Divide in 4 equal sections and form patties. Bake for 7 to 10 minutes. Carefully flip and bake until crusty on the outside for extra 10 minutes.
5. Place on a whole grain bun with your favorite toppings.

Nutrition per serving:

Total Calories: 118, Total Fat: 1g, Saturated Fat: 0g, Cholesterol: 7mg, Sodium: 108mg, Potassium: 583mg, Total Carbs: 21g, Fiber: 7g, Sugars: 0g, Protein: 7g

5.10 Baked Sweet Potatoes with Cumin

Serves: 4 | Preparation Time: 15 minutes | Cooking Time: 20 minutes

Ingredients:

- sweet potatoes - 4
- Freshly ground black pepper – ¼ tsp.
- diced red onion - ½
- low-fat or nonfat plain Greek yogurt - ½ c.
- olive oil - 1 tsp.
- diced and cored red bell pepper - 1
- ground cumin - 1 tsp.
- drained and rinsed chickpeas - 1 (15 oz.) can

Procedure:

1. Prick the potatoes using a fork and cook on potato setting of the microwave for 10 minutes until well cooked and potatoes become soft.
2. Using a bowl, add in black pepper and yogurt and combine. Set a pot over a medium source of heat, add in oil and heat. Add in cumin, bell pepper, onion and an extra black pepper to enhance the taste.

3. Add in the chickpeas, stir well to combine, and allow the mixture to cook for 5 minutes. Slice potatoes midway lengthwise down and top each half with a portion of the bean mixture followed by 1 to 2 tbsps. of the yogurt. Serve immediately.

Nutrition per serving:

Calories: 264, Fat: 2g, Sodium: 124mg, Carbs: 51g, Protein: 12g, Potassium: 78mg.

5.11 White Beans with Spinach and Pan-Roasted Tomatoes

Serves: 2 | Preparation Time: 15 minutes | Time: 11 minutes

Ingredients:

- olive oil - 1 tbsp.
- halved plum tomatoes - 4
- frozen spinach, defrosted and squeezed of excess water - 10 oz.
- thinly sliced garlic cloves - 2
- water - 2 tbsps.
- black pepper, freshly ground - ¼ tsp.
- drained white beans - 1 can
- Juice from 1 lemon

Procedure:

1. Add and heat oil in your nonstick skillet set over a medium high source of heat. Add tomatoes, the cut-side should face down, and let cook within 5 minutes. You then flip to the second side and cook within 1 more minute. Set on a plate.
2. Lower your heat towards medium setting and mix in spinach, pepper, water, and garlic. Cook as you toss for 3 minutes to ensure the spinach is cooked through.
3. Take back the tomatoes to your skillet, add the white beans and lemon juice, toss well until heated for 2 minutes.

Nutrition per serving:

Calories: 293, Fat: 9g, Sodium: 267mg, Carbs: 43g, Protein: 15g, Potassium: 78mg.

5.12 Black-Eyed Peas and Greens Power Salad

Serves: 2 | Preparation Time: 15 minutes | Cooking Time: 6 minutes

Ingredients:

- olive oil - 1 tbsp.
- Juice of ½ lemon
- chopped purple cabbage - 3 c.
- baby spinach - 5 c.
- Salt – ¼ tsp.
- shredded carrots - 1 c.
- drained black-eyed peas - 1 can
- Ground black pepper – ¼ tsp.

Procedure:

1. In a medium pan, add oil and cabbage and sauté for 2 minutes while on the medium heat setting. Add in your spinach, cook for 4 minutes while covered until the greens become wilted. Once done, transfer to a bowl.
2. Mix in peas, carrots, juice, pepper and salt as you toss well.

Nutrition per serving:

Calories: 320, Fat: 9g, Sodium: 351mg, Potassium: 544mg, Carbs: 49g, Protein: 16g.

5.13 Butternut-Squash Macaroni and Cheese

Serves: 2 | Preparation Time: 15 min | Cooking Time: 20 minutes

Ingredients:

- ziti macaroni, whole-wheat - 1 c.
- olive oil - 1 tbsp.
- cubed butternut squash, peeled - 2 c.
- nonfat divide milk - 1 c.
- black pepper - ¼ tsp.
- Dijon mustard - 1 tsp.
- shredded low-fat cheddar cheese - ¼ c.

Procedure:

1. Cook your pasta al dente using a pot with boiling water. Drain pasta and place aside. Using a saucepan set on a medium high source of heat, mix ½ c. milk and butternut squash. Add black pepper for seasoning. Allow to simmer. Reduce heat intensity and continue cooking for 10 minutes.
2. Using a blender, mix in Dijon mustard and squash. Purée well to obtain a smooth consistency. Meanwhile, using a sauté pan set on medium heat, mix in olive oil, the squash purée and the rest of the milk. Simmer for 5 minutes before stirring in the cheese.
3. Add in your pasta as you stir. Enjoy right away.

Nutrition per serving:

Calories: 373, Fat: 10g, Sodium: 193mg, Carbs: 59g, Protein: 14g, Potassium: 56mg.

5.14 Pasta with Peas & Tomatoes

Serves: 2 | Preparation Time: 15 minutes | Cooking Time: 15 minutes

Ingredients:

- whole-grain pasta of choice - ½ c.
- water - 8 c. plus ¼ for finishing
- frozen peas - 1 c.
- olive oil - 1 tbsp.
- halved cherry tomatoes - 1 c.
- Ground black pepper - ¼ tsp.

- dried basil - 1 tsp.
- grated Parmesan cheese (low-sodium) - ¼ c.

Procedure:

1. Cook your pasta accordingly until al dente. Add the water to the same pot you used to cook the pasta, and when it's boiling, add the peas. Cook within 5 minutes before draining and setting aside until ready.
2. Using a nonstick skillet set over medium source of heat. Pour in oil and heat. Mix in cherry tomatoes, set lid in place and allow the tomatoes to soften for 5 minutes as you occasionally stir.
3. Add in basil and black pepper for seasoning. Toss in peas, pasta, and ¼ cup of water, stir and remove from heat. Enjoy with a topping of Parmesan.

Nutrition per serving:

Calories: 266, Fat: 12g, Sodium: 320mg, Carbs: 30g, Protein: 13g, Potassium: 67mg.

5.15 Healthy Vegetable Fried Rice

Serves: 4 | Preparation Time: 15 minutes | Cooking Time: 10 minutes

Ingredients:

For sauce:

- garlic vinegar - 1/3 c.
- dark molasses - 1½ tbsps.
- onion powder - 1 tsp.

For the fried rice:

- olive oil - 1 tsp.
- lightly beaten whole eggs - 2 + 4 egg whites
- frozen mixed vegetables - 1 c.
- frozen edamame - 1 c.
- cooked brown rice - 2 c.

Procedure:

1. To prepare sauce, mix the garlic vinegar, molasses, and onion powder in a glass jar. Shake well.
2. Using a skillet set over a medium high source of heat, add in oil and heat. Set in eggs and egg whites, cook for 1 minute until the eggs set.
3. Use a spoon to break eggs into small pieces. Mix in edamame and mixed vegetables. Cook as you stir for approximately 4 minutes.
4. Mix in the sauce and brown rice to your veggie-egg mixture and cook until well done for 5 minutes. Serve immediately.

Nutrition per serving:

Calories: 210, Fat: 6g, Sodium: 113mg, Carbs: 28g, Protein: 13g, Potassium: 78mg.

5.16 Cast Iron Roots and Grain

Serves: 4 | Preparation Time: 10 minutes | Cooking Time: 30 minutes

Ingredients:

- olive oil - 2 tbsps.
- honey - 2 tsps.
- sliced rainbow carrots - 2 c.
- sliced beets - 1 c.
- chopped turnips - 1 c.
- sliced onion - 1 c.
- fresh tarragon - 1 tbsp.
- dried lavender - 1 tsp.
- low sodium vegetable broth - 4 c.
- bulgur - 1 ½ c.

Procedure:

1. Set a cast iron skillet over a medium high source of heat and heat well.
2. Using a bowl, combine the beets, turnips, carrots, and onion. Drizzle over the honey and olive oil. Add tarragon and lavender for seasoning. Toss well to ensure well coated.
3. Add the vegetables to your skillet and cook until slightly tender, approximately 10 minutes.
4. Mix in vegetable broth and allow to boil.
5. Mix in the bulgur and reduce your heat to low. Simmer for 15 minutes while covered until bulgur becomes tender.

Nutritional Information:

Calories 312.1, Total fat 7.6 g, saturated fat 1.0 g, Sodium 241.4 mg, potassium 593.8 mg, Total carbs 56.4 g, dietary fiber 13.9 g, Sugars 10.8 g, protein 7.9 g

5.17 Easy Beet and Goat Cheese Risotto

Serves: 4 | Preparation Time: 10 minutes | Cooking Time: 30 minutes

Ingredients:

- olive oil - ¼ c.
- diced beets - 1 ½ c.
- diced red onion - 1 c.
- chopped spinach - 2 c.
- Arborio rice - 1 c.
- low sodium vegetable broth - 2 c.
- chopped fresh rosemary - 2 tsps.
- goat cheese - ½ c.
- chopped walnuts - ¼ c.

Procedure:

1. Using a saucepan set over a medium source of heat, add olive oil and heat.
2. Add in onions and beets. Sauté until tender, approximately 5 minutes.
3. Mix in spinach and cook for 3 more minutes.
4. Add in rice and continue cooking as you stir for 3 minutes, to lightly toast the rice.

5. Next, add the vegetable broth and rosemary. Increase the heat to ensure the broth boils.
6. Reduce your heat intensity to low, and continue cooking as you stir occasionally, until the rice has a soft but firm texture.
7. Take out from the heat and stir in goat cheese.
8. Garnish with chopped walnuts for serving.

Nutritional Information:

Calories 412.5, Total fat 29.2 g, saturated fat 6.0 g, Sodium 257.3 mg, potassium 352.7 mg, Total carbs 26.7 g, dietary fiber 4.5 g, Sugars 16.9 g, protein 11.1 g

5.18 Mushroom and Eggplant Casserole

Serves: 4 | Preparation Time: 10 minutes | Cooking Time: 30 minutes

Ingredients:

- sliced eggplant - 1 pound
- olive oil - 1 tbsp.
- chopped yellow onion - 1 c.
- crushed and minced cloves garlic - 3
- oregano - 1 tsp.
- black pepper - ½ tsp.
- sliced mushrooms - 3 c.
- tomato sauce (low sodium) - 1 c.
- cooked brown rice - 2 c.
- low fat mozzarella cheese - 1 c.
- grated asiago cheese - ½ c.
- fresh chopped basil - ¼ c.

Procedure:

1. Preheat your oven to attain 375°F.
2. Using a nonstick skillet set on medium high heat intensity, pour in olive oil and heat.
3. Mix in the eggplant and cook each side for 3 minutes. Place aside.
4. Add in the garlic, oregano, onion, and black pepper to the pan. Sauté for 4 minutes until onions become tender. Add the mushrooms and cook an additional 3 minutes.
5. Lightly oil an 8x8 baking dish and spread along the bottom a thin layer of tomato sauce.
6. Make layers of eggplant, rice, mozzarella, and mushrooms, repeating until all ingredients have been used.
7. Make the final layer mozzarella topped with asiago cheese and fresh basil.
8. Set in your oven and bake for 20 minutes.

Nutritional Information:

Calories 377.7, Total fat 16.1 g, saturated fat 8.2 g, Sodium 383.0 mg, potassium 604.4 mg, Total carbs 41.1 g, dietary fiber 6.2 g, Sugars 4.5 g, protein 19.6 g

5.19 Spinach Soufflés

Serves: 4 | Preparation time: 15 minutes | Cooking time: 1 hour & 20 minutes

Ingredients

- egg whites - 4
- Dried parsley - 1 tsp.
- Cream of tartar - ¼ tsp.
- Whole-wheat bread crumbs - 1 tbsp. + 1 ½ tsp.
- Minced garlic - 1 tsp.
- Parmesan cheese - 2 oz.
- Baby spinach - 6 oz.
- All-purpose flour - 2 tbsps.
- Black pepper - 1/8 tsp.
- egg yolks - 2

Procedure:

9. Let your oven preheat to attain 425 F.
10. Oil spray 4 ramekins of six oz. and sprinkle with crumbs on all sides.
11. Using a bowl, whisk together tartar and egg.
12. Oil spray a pan and sauté garlic and spinach for 4 minutes. Turn off heat and add parsley.
13. In a pan, add flour, milk and black pepper, whisk well and allow it to boil, simmer as you keep whisking for 5 minutes. Let it cool.
14. Whisk the egg white to medium peaks.
15. In the milk mixture, add spinach mixture, add yolks, parmesan and mix.
16. Fold in egg whites in batches. Pour in the prepared ramekins, tap to get the excess air out and set on a baking tray.
17. Let bake for 5 minutes, change temperature to 350 F, Bake for an extra 20 minutes. Enjoy.

Nutrition per serving:

Calories 144, Fat 6.0 g, Sugar 3 g, Protein 14 g, Sodium 354 mg, Carbs 9 g

5.20 Huevos Rancheros

Serves: 4 | Preparation time: 15 minutes | Cooking time: 25 minutes

Ingredients:

- Diced onion - ½ c.
- Canned crushed tomatoes, fire-roasted - 15 oz.
- Water - 2 tbsps.
- deseeded and diced poblano pepper - ½ c.
- Canola oil - 1 tsp.
- fresh jalapeño pepper - 1
- Minced garlic - 1 ½ tsps.

For Huevos

- avocado cut in fours - 1
- canola oil - 1 tsp.
- corn tortillas (6") - 4
- eggs - 4
- rinsed black beans - 1 (15 oz.) can

- shredded & low-fat Mexican blend cheese - ¼ c.

Procedure:

18. In a sizable pan, add oil and heat on medium flame, sauté your onion for about 2 minutes.
19. Mix in peppers and cook for 2 more minutes. Add in garlic. Continue cooking for an extra 1 minute.
20. Add water, salt and tomatoes, let it boil, reduce heat to low and let simmer for about 5 minutes. Take from heat and keep warm.
21. Using a skillet, add oil and cook egg for 4 minutes.
22. For each tortilla, add eggs and beans, tomato salsa, and the rest of the ingredients.
23. Roll and enjoy.

Nutrition per serving:

Calories 334, Fat 13.5 g, Sugar 9 g, Protein 17 g, Sodium 265 mg, Carbs 37 g

5.21 Eggplant Special

Serves: 6 | Preparation time: 15 minutes | Cooking time: 1 hour & 40 minutes

Ingredients:

- eggs - 2
- Water - 2 tbsps.
- whole-wheat panko breadcrumbs - 1 c.
- torn fresh basil - ¼ c.
- eggplants sliced into ¼" thick slices - 2 pounds
- Italian seasoning - 1 tsp.
- minced garlic cloves - 2
- Black pepper - ½ tsp.
- Tomato sauce, unsalted - 1 (24 oz.) jar
- Red pepper flakes - ½ tsp.

Procedure:

24. Let your oven preheat to attain 400 F.
25. Oil spray a baking dish.
26. Using a bowl, add in egg and water and whisk.
27. Using a dish, add Italian seasoning and bread crumbs.
28. Coat eggplant in whisked egg, then in bread crumbs, press to adhere.
29. Set breaded eggplant on the prepared baking sheet. Oil spray your eggplant on both sides.
30. Bake for half an hour, switch racks after flipping the eggplant in the upper and third rack.
31. Sprinkle pepper.
32. Using a bowl, add in garlic, tomato sauce, red pepper, and basil. Mix.
33. In the baking dish, add half a cup of the sauce, place the eggplant slices and add one cup of sauce on top.
34. Bake for 30 minutes, cool for about 5 minutes. Enjoy.

Nutrition per serving:

Calories 241, Fat 9 g, Sugar 9 g, Protein 14 g, Sodium 487 mg, Carbs 28 g

5.22 Zucchini Black Bean Tacos

Serves: 4 | Preparation time: 20 minutes | Cooking time: 0 minutes

Ingredients:

- Salsa, as needed

For tacos

- Chili powder - ½ tsp.
- corn tortillas - 8
- Chipotle powder - ½ tsp.
- rinsed Black beans - 1 (15 oz.) can
- Paprika - ¼ tsp.
- Garlic powder - ¼ tsp.
- zucchini, grated - 1

Avocado Crema (blend all ingredients)

- Greek yogurt, low-fat - ½ c.
- avocado - 1
- Juice of 1 lime

Procedure:

35. Using a bowl, add all the taco ingredients, except for tortillas.
36. Warm the tortillas in the oven.
37. Add the taco mix, salsa and avocado crema on top.
38. Enjoy.

Nutrition per serving:

Calories 245, Fat 10 g, Sugar 5 g, Protein 6.4 g, Sodium 321 mg, Carbs 35 g

5.23 Polenta Squares with Cheese & Pine Nuts

Serves: 30 | Preparation Time: 20 minutes + Cooling | Cooking Time: 40 minutes

Ingredients:

- Quick-cooking polenta - 1 c.
- Crumbled gorgonzola cheese, low-fat - 1/3 c.
- Unsalted butter - 1 tbsp.
- boiling water - ¼ c.
- water - 4 c.
- balsamic vinegar - ⅔ c.
- Toasted pine nuts - 3 tbsps.
- Flat-leaf chopped fresh parsley - 2 tbsps.
- Grated zest - 1 tsp.
- Currants - 3 tbsps.

Procedure:

39. In a pan, add water (4 cups) and boil; slowly add polenta while whisking.
40. Whisk on low flame for 4 minutes till it thickens.
41. Add butter and pour in an oil sprayed baking pan (square-9").

42. Cover with plastic wrap on top; it should touch the polenta surface, keep in the fridge for 60 minutes. Slice in 30 squares.
43. In your bowl, mix currants with boiling water (1/4 cup). Let it rest for 10 minutes draining.
44. Using a bowl, add currants, zest, pine nuts, and cheese.
45. In a pan, add vinegar, cook on medium heat for ten minutes, until reduced by 2 tbsp. Let it cool.
46. Using a skillet set over a medium source of heat, add oil and heat. Mix in polenta squares and cook one side for 6 minutes.
47. Serve with cheese mixture and drizzle of vinegar.

Nutrition per serving:

Calories 130, Fat 1.1 g, Sugar 8 g, Protein 3.1 g, Sodium 201 mg, Carbs 18 g

6 VEGAN PLATES

6.1 Vegetarian Black Bean Pasta

Serves: 6 | Preparation time: 15 minutes | Cooking time: 20 minutes

Ingredients

- sliced Portobello baby mushrooms - 1 ¾ c.
- Olive oil - 1 tsp.
- Diced tomatoes with juices - 1 (15 oz.) can
- minced garlic clove - 1
- Whole wheat fettuccine - 9 oz.
- Baby spinach - 2 c.
- Dried rosemary - 1 tsp.
- rinsed Black beans - 1 (15 oz.) can
- Dried oregano - ½ tsp.

Procedure:

1. Cook pasta as per the pack's instructions.
2. Set a skillet over a medium source of heat. Add oil and heat. Mix in mushrooms to sauté and cook for 6 minutes.
3. Add in garlic and continue cooking for 1 minute.
4. Mix in the remaining ingredients, toss well and enjoy.

Nutrition for 1 ¼ cups:

Calories 255, Fat 3 g, Sugar 4 g, Protein 12 g, Sodium 230 mg, Carbs 45 g

6.2 Lentil Medley

Serves: 8 | Prep Time: 20 minutes | Cook Time: 25 min

Ingredients:

- water - 2 c.
- diced red onion - 1
- sliced mushrooms - 2 c.
- Lentils - 1 c.
- cubed zucchini - 1
- Soft sun-dried tomato (not in oil) - ½ c.
- Fresh mint - ¼ c.
- Olive oil - 3 tbsps.
- cubed cucumber - 1
- Dried oregano - 1 tsp.
- Honey - 2 tsps.
- Rice vinegar - ½ c.
- chopped Baby spinach - 4 c.
- Dried basil - 1 tsp.

Procedure:

1. Cook lentils in water after rinsing for 25 minutes. Use cold water for draining and rinsing once again.
2. Transfer to a mixing bowl, mix in the remaining ingredients, toss and serve.

Nutrition per serving:

Calories 225 | Fat 8 g | Sugar 11 g | Protein 6.4 g |Sodium 400 mg | Carbs 29 g

6.3 Zucchini with Corn

Serves: 6 | Preparation time: 20 minutes | Cooking time: 20 minutes

Ingredients:

- Olive oil - 1 tbsp.
- Diced onion - 1/4 c.
- zucchinis cut into ¼" thick slices - 3
- Fresh corn kernels - 4 c.
- Black pepper - ¼ tsp.
- minced garlic clove - 1
- fresh jalapeño, chopped without seeds - 1
- Salt - 1/8 tsp.

Procedure:

1. Set corn in water and boil, cook for 10 mins on low, cover, then drain.
2. In hot oil, add onion and garlic. Sauté for 5 minutes before adding zucchini and cook for an extra 5 minutes.
3. Add jalapenos, pepper, corn and pepper, cook for ten minutes.
4. Turn the heat off and serve.

Nutrition per serving:

Calories 202, Fat 5 g, Sugar 8 g, Protein 7 g, Sodium 164 mg, Carbs 40 g

6.4 Couscous with Beans & Vegetables

Serves: 6 | Preparation time: 20 minutes | Cooking time: 20 minutes

Ingredients:

- diced onion - 1
- red bell pepper cut into thin strips - 1
- sliced carrot - 1
- Olive oil - 2 tsps.
- Vegetable broth, low-fat - 1 c.
- zucchini cut into half-moons - 1
- celery rib, sliced - 1
- tomato, diced - 1
- Minced garlic - 1 tsp.
- Red kidney beans, rinsed - 2 (16 oz.) cans
- cubed sweet potato - 1
- Dried thyme - 1 tsp.
- Salt - 1/8 tsp.

- Ground cumin - 1 tsp.
- Minced parsley - ¼ c.
- Paprika - ½ tsp.
- Cayenne - 1/8 tsp.
- Whole-wheat couscous - 1 c.

Procedure:

1. Using a skillet set on a medium source of heat, add oil and heat. Sauté all vegetables for 5 minutes before adding garlic and cooking for approximately 30 seconds.
2. Mix in the rest of the ingredients, except for couscous, let it come to a simple boil while on high heat setting, turn the heat to low intensity then allow for simmering to take place for 15 minutes.
3. Cook couscous as per pack's instruction.
4. Serve the vegetables with fluffed couscous.

Nutrition per serving:

Calories 330, Fat 2.5 g, Sugar 8 g, Protein 16 g, Sodium 241 mg, Carbs 65 g

6.5 Roasted Kabocha with Wild Rice

Serves: 4 | Preparation Time: 20 minutes | Cooking Time: 2 hours

Ingredients:

- Olive oil - ¼ c.
- Chili powder - 1 tsp.
- Black pepper - ¼ tsp.
- Wild rice - ½ c.
- Kabocha squash - 3 pounds
- Pumpkin seeds - ½ c.
- Pomegranate seeds - ½ c.
- chopped fresh parsley, - ¼ c.
- Lime juice - 1 tbsp.
- Honey - 1 tsp.
- Lime zest - 1 tsp.

Procedure:

1. Let the oven preheat to 375 F.
2. With a fork, pierce the squash all over and place it on a baking sheet with aluminium foil.
3. Allow to roast for about 80 minutes.
4. Cut the squash into 5-6 pieces lengthwise. Take the middle part out.
5. Season the squash with oil (1 tbsp.) and sprinkles of pepper; set on your baking sheet flesh side up.
6. Broil the squash for 5-7 minutes.
7. In a skillet, add pumpkin seeds and oil (1 tbsp.) and allow to cook for 3 minutes. Mix in honey and chili powder, and continue cooking for 30 seconds. Take them out on a plate and cool.
8. Using a pan, add in water (1 ½ cups), and let it boil. Add rice and let boil, turn heat to low and let simmer for 25 minutes while covered, drain.

9. Using a bowl, add rice, pumpkin seeds, zest, juice, parsley, oil (2 tbsp.), and toss well.
10. Serve with broiled squash on top.

Nutrition per serving:

Calories 250, Fat 17.2 g, Sugar 8 g, Protein 6.4 g, Sodium 155 mg, Carbs

6.6 Acorn Squash & Coconut Creamed Greens Casserole

Serves: 4 | Preparation Time: 20 minutes | Cooking Time: 2 hours

Ingredients:

- coconut milk - 1 (15 oz.) can
- minced jalapeno without seeds - ½
- Grapeseed oil - 2 tbsps.
- Cornstarch - 1 tbsp.
- Chopped ginger - 2 tbsps.
- minced garlic cloves - 4
- Black pepper - ¼ tsp.
- Lime juice - 1 tbsp.
- diced plum tomatoes - 2
- chopped sweet onion - 1
- Light agave syrup - 1 tsp.
- packed and chopped Tuscan kale - 10 c.
- Ground cumin - 2 tsps.
- Acorn squash sliced into 1/8" of thickness - 1 ¼ pounds
- packed Swiss chard, chopped - 7 c.

Procedure:

1. Let the oven preheat to 425 F. mix coconut milk with the cornstarch.
2. Using a skillet set on medium source of heat, add and heat oil. Sauté onion for about 4 minutes.
3. Mix in garlic, ginger, jalapenos and continue cooking for 2 more minutes; add black pepper.
4. Add tomato to the onion mixture. Cook until done for 2 minutes, mix in cumin and cook for an additional 1 minute.
5. Add kale and chard before cooking to wilt and the liquid evaporates.
6. Add agave syrup and coconut milk. Let it simmer and cook the mixture for 3 minutes.
7. Add lime juice.
8. Into a baking dish (8 by 10"), add the creamed greens, add squash on top.
9. Bake for 25-30 minutes. Enjoy.

Nutrition per serving:

Calories 248, Fat 17.2 g, Sugar 8 g, Protein 11 g, Sodium 164 mg, Carbs 33 g

6.7 Warm Spiced Cabbage Bake

Serves: 4 | Preparation Time: 20 minutes | Cooking Time: 60 minutes

Ingredients:

- chopped raisins - 2 tbsps.
- Black pepper - ¼ tsp.
- chopped fresh dill - ½ c.
- chopped and toasted pine nuts - 1/3 c.
- Olive oil - 5 tbsps.
- Savoy cabbage (6 wedges) - 1 ½ pounds
- chopped sweet onion - 1
- sliced garlic cloves - 4
- Whole tomatoes, peeled & crushed - 1 (15 oz.) can
- Allspice - A pinch
- Sweet paprika - 1 tsp.
- low-fat vegan Sour cream - ½ c.
- Ground cinnamon - ¼ tsp.
- Red pepper flakes - ¼ tsp.
- Salt – a pinch

Procedure:

1. Let your oven preheat to attain 400 F.
2. Using a bowl, add dill, nuts and raisins and mix together.
3. Using a skillet set on a medium high source of heat, add 2 tbsp. of oil. Cook cabbage wedges for 5-6 minutes on both sides, take it out on a plate and sprinkle black pepper.
4. Add the remaining oil in the skillet, sauté garlic and onion on low flame for 4 minutes.
5. Mix in spices and continue cooking for 1 more minute.
6. Mix in water (1 cup) and tomatoes, add the nut mixture (half). Let it simmer and add salt to season.
7. Add your cabbage wedges to skillet and set in oven before baking for half an hour.
8. Serve with the rest of the nut mixture and sour cream topping.

Nutrition per serving:

Calories 131, Fat 3 g, Sugar 3 g, Protein 21 g, Sodium 145 mg, Carbs 6 g

6.8 Curried Cauliflower with Chickpeas

Serves: 4 | Preparation Time: 20 minutes | Cooking Time: 75 minutes

Ingredients:

- Dried chickpeas, rinsed - 3/4 c.
- Minced ginger - 2 tbsps.
- Canola oil - 2 tsps.
- chopped onion - 1
- water - 3 c.
- cauliflower broken into florets - 1 medium head
- diced red bell pepper - 1

- minced garlic cloves - 3
- Curry powder - 2 tbsps.
- Salt - 1/8 tsp.
- Vegetable broth, low-sodium - 1 ½ c.

Procedure:

1. Cook chickpeas in a pressure cooker with water for 45 minutes on high pressure.
2. Let the pressure release naturally for 15 minutes, drain.
3. Sauté onion in hot oil for 3 minutes, add bell pepper and cook for 3 more minutes.
4. Mix in ginger and garlic, cook for 30 seconds.
5. In the pressure cooker, add cauliflower, salt, broth and curry powder. Add chickpeas with sautéed vegetables, cook on high pressure setting for 3 minutes. Release pressure quickly. Serve.

Nutrition per serving:

Calories 224, Fat 5.5 g, Sugar 10 g, Protein 11 g, Sodium 201 mg, Carbs 37 g

7 SIDES AND SMALL PLATES

7.1 Soy Sauce Green Beans

Serves: 12 | Preparation Time: 10 minutes | Cooking Time: 2 hours

Ingredients:

- olive oil - 3 tbsps.
- green beans - 16 oz. (455g)
- garlic powder - 1/2 tsp.
- coconut sugar - 1/2 c.
- low-sodium soy sauce - 1 tsp.

Procedure:

1. Using a slow cooker, add in soy sauce, green beans, sugar, oil, and garlic powder. Mix well before covering and allowing to cook for 2 hours on "low".
2. Toss well before dividing in serving plates and enjoy your side dish.

Nutrition per serving:

46 calories, 0.8g proteins, 3.6g carbs (0.6g sugars), 3.6g fats, 29mg sodium, 80mg potassium

7.2 Sour Cream Green Beans

Serves: 8 | Preparation Time: 10 minutes | Cooking Time: 4 hours

Ingredients:

- green beans - 15 oz.
- corn - 14 oz.
- sliced mushrooms - 4 oz.
- cream of mushroom soup, low-fat and sodium-free - 11 oz
- low-fat sour cream - 1/2 c.
- chopped almonds - 1/2 c.
- low-fat cheddar cheese, shredded - 1/2 c.

Procedure:

1. Using a slow cooker, add in all ingredients and mix. Toss well and cook for 4 hours on low setting while covered.
2. Stir again one extra time. Set in serving plates and enjoy.

Nutrition per serving:

360 calories, 14g proteins, 58.3g carbs (10.3g sugars), 12.7g fats, 220mg sodium, 967mg potassium, 10g fibers, 14mg cholesterol

7.3 Cumin Brussels Sprouts

Serves: 4 | Preparation Time: 10 minutes | Cooking Time: 3 hours

Ingredients:

- low-sodium veggie stock - 1 c.
- Brussels sprouts, trimmed and halved - 1 pound
- rosemary, dried - 1 tsp.

- cumin, ground - 1 tsp.
- mint, chopped - 1 tbsp.

Procedure:

1. Using a slow cooker, combine all the above ingredients. Set a lid in place and cook for 3 hours on "low".
2. Divide in serving plates and enjoy your side dish.

Nutrition per serving:

56 calories, 4g proteins, 11.4g carbs (2.7g sugars), 0.6g fats, 65mg sodium, 460mg potassium, 4.5g fibers

7.4 Peach And Carrots

Serves: 6 | Preparation Time: 10 minutes | Cooking Time: 6 hours

Ingredients:

- peeled small carrots - 2 pounds
- cinnamon powder - 1/2 tsp.
- melted low-fat butter - 1/2 c.
- canned peach, unsweetened - 1/2 c.
- cornstarch - 2 tbsps.
- stevia - 3 tbsps.
- water - 2 tbsps.
- vanilla extract - 1 tsp.
- ground nutmeg - A pinch

Procedure:

1. Using a slow cooker, mix in all the above ingredients. Toss well before you cover and cook for 6 hours on "low".
2. Toss again one more time before setting in serving plates and enjoy your side dish.

Nutrition per serving:

139 calories, 3.8g proteins, 35.4g carbs (6.9g sugars), 10.7g fats, 199mg sodium, 25mg potassium, 4.2g fibers

7.5 Chive & Garlic "Mash"

Serves: 2 | Preparation Time: 8 minutes | Cooking Time: 20 minutes

Ingredients:

- vegetable stock - 2 c.
- peeled Yukon potatoes - 2 pound
- peeled cloves garlic - 4
- almond milk - ½ c.
- flavored vinegar - ½ tsp.
- chopped chives - ¼ c.

Procedure:

1. Using an instant pot, add in potatoes, garlic and broth.
2. Cook for 9 minutes on HIGH pressure setting while the lid is locked.
3. Naturally release pressure for about 10 minutes

4. Drain and keep the appropriate liquid that will maintain the required consistency.
5. You then mash your potatoes. Add in milk, chives and vinegar as you stir.
6. Enjoy!

Nutrition per serving:

292 Calories, 15g Fat, 34g Carbs, 7g Protein, 123mg Potassium, 82mg Sodium

7.6 Spiced Broccoli Florets

Serves: 10 | Preparation Time: 10 minutes | Cooking Time: 3 hours

Procedure:

- broccoli florets - 6 c.
- low-fat shredded cheddar cheese - 1 ½ c.
- cider vinegar - ½ tsp.
- chopped yellow onion - ¼ c.
- tomato sauce, sodium-free - 10 oz.
- olive oil - 2 tbsps.
- black pepper - A pinch

Procedure:

1. Apply oil to your slow cooker for greasing. Mix in vinegar, broccoli, black pepper, tomato sauce and onion. Cook on high setting for 2½ hours on "high" while covered.
2. Sprinkle cheese over your mixture, cover again and let cook for 30 more minutes on "high". Set in serving plates and enjoy your side dish.

Nutrition per serving:

119 calories, 6.2g proteins, 5.7g carbs (2.3g sugars), 8.7g fats, 272mg sodium, 288mg potassium, 18mg cholesterol, 1.9g fibers

7.7 Mashed Cauliflower with Garlic

Serves: 4 | Preparation Time: 5 minutes | Cooking Time: 25 minutes

Ingredients:

- non-hydrogenated soft-bowl margarine - 1 tbsp.
- cauliflower - 1 head
- leek split into 4 parts, white only - 1
- clove garlic - 1
- Pepper - ¼ tsp.

Procedure:

1. Break up little bits of cauliflower. Steam the garlic, leeks, and cauliflower in water in a saucepan until they become tender for 25 minutes.
2. Using a food processor, add the vegetables and puree well to get a mashed potato-like texture. You can process in small portions at a given time.

3. Using a mixer if you want a finer finish. With a dishtowel, make sure to tightly keep the blender cap on. If the vegetables tend to be dusty, add some more hot water.
4. As per your taste, stir in margarine and pepper. Just serve.

Nutrition per serving:

Calories: 217, Fat: 5g, Fiber: 8g, Sugars 12g, Protein: 4g, Sodium: 25mg, Potassium: 276mg

7.8 Chinese-Style Asparagus

Serves: 2 | Preparation Time: 15 minutes | Cooking Time: 4 minutes

Ingredients:

- water - ½ c.
- soy sauce, reduced-sodium - 1 tsp.
- sugar - ½ tsp.
- fresh asparagus, remove woody ends and slice into 1 ½ inch pieces - 1½ pounds

Procedure:

1. Using a saucepan set over a medium high source of heat, mix in soy sauce, sugar and water and heat. Allow to get to boiling point before adding asparagus. Lower the heat intensity and let boil on low for 4 minutes until the asparagus becomes crispy and tender.
2. Set in serving bowls to serve.

Nutrition per serving:

Calories: 260, Fat: 5g, Carbs: 20g, Protein: 22g, Sodium: 89mg, Potassium: 695mg

7.9 Fresh Fruit Kebabs

Serves: 8 | Preparation Time: 35 minutes | Cooking Time: 0 minutes

Ingredients:

- low-fat lemon yogurt, sugar-free - 6 oz.
- lime juice, fresh - 1 tsp.
- pineapple chunks each ½ inch in size - 4
- red grapes - 4
- lime zest - 1 tsp.
- strawberries - 4
- peeled and quartered kiwi - 1
- banana, sliced into 4 ½" chunks - ½
- wooden skewers - 4

Procedure:

1. Using a shallow dish, add in lime zest, lime juice, and yogurt and whisk. Set in your refrigerator while covered until when ready for use.
2. To each of the skewers, thread each fruit. Serve alongside your lemon-lime dip.

Nutrition per serving:

Calories: 27, Fat: 10g, Carbs: 20g, Protein: 10g, Sodium: 3mg, Potassium: 138mg

7.10 Pomegranate And Ricotta Bruschetta

Serves: 8 | Preparation Time: 12 minutes | Cooking Time: 12 minutes

Ingredients:

- Grated lemon zest - 1/2 tsp.
- sliced Nut Bread, Whole Grain - 6
- Ricotta Cheese Low Fat - 1 c.
- Pomegranate Arils - 1/2 c.
- Fresh thyme - 2 tsps.

Procedure:

1. Toast your bread to brown lightly.
2. In the meantime, use a bowl to whisk lemon zest and cheese.
3. Slice halfway the toasted bread. Spread cottage cheese to the top.
4. Add a topping of pomegranate and thyme.
5. Enjoy.

Nutrition per serving:

Calories per Serving 69, Protein: 4.1g, Carbs: 11.1g, Fat: 1.0g, Saturated Fat: 0.2g, Sodium: 123mg, Potassium: 427mg

7.11 Carrot Sticks with Onion and Sour Cream

Serves: 8 | Preparation Time: 10 minutes | Cooking Time: 0 minutes

Ingredients:

- carrot sticks - 2 c.
- peeled and minced sweet onion - 1
- mayonnaise low fat - 2 tbsps.
- sour cream - ½ c.
- stalks celery, chopped - 4

Procedure:

1. Using a bowl, add in mayonnaise and sour cream. Whisk well to combine.
2. Add in onion and stir.
3. Set in the refrigerator for 1 hour and enjoy with carrot sticks and celery.

Nutrition per serving:

Calories per Serving: 60, Protein: 1.6g, Carbs: 7.2g, Fat: 3.1g, Saturated Fat: 1.7g, Sodium: 38 mg, Potassium: 577mg

7.12 Parsley Fennel

Serves: 4 | Preparation Time: 10 minutes| Cooking Time: 2h 30 minutes

Ingredients:

- avocado oil - 2 tsps.
- fennel bulbs, sliced - 2
- turmeric powder - 1/2 tsp.
- chopped parsley - 1 tbsp.

- Juice and zest of 1 lime
- veggie stock, low-sodium - 1/4 c.

Procedure:

1. In your slow cooker, add in and mix all the above ingredients and let cook for 2 ½ hours on LOW setting while covered.
2. Enjoy your side dish.

Nutrition per serving:

Calories 47, Fat 0.6g, Cholesterol 0mg, Sodium 71mg, Carbs 10.8g, Fiber 4.3g| Sugars 0.4g, Protein 1.7g, Potassium 521mg

7.13 Parsley Red Potatoes

Serves: 8 | Preparation Time: 10 min | Cooking Time: 6 hours

Ingredients:

- halved baby red potatoes - 16
- olive oil - 2 tbsps.
- chicken stock, low-sodium - 2 c.
- sliced carrot - 1
- chopped yellow onion - 1/4 c.
- chopped celery rib - 1
- black pepper - A pinch
- chopped parsley - 1 tbsp.
- minced garlic clove - 1

Procedure:

1. Using a slow cooker, add in potatoes, carrot, onion, garlic, black pepper, oil, stock, celery, and parsley. Toss well and cook for 6 hours on low setting while covered.
2. Set in serving plates and enjoy your side dish.

Nutrition per serving:

Calories 256, Fat 9.6g, Cholesterol 0mg, Sodium 846mg, Carbs 43.5g, Fiber 4.5g, Sugars 4.7g, Protein 4.5g, Potassium 48mg

7.14 Italians Style Mushroom Mix

Serves: 6 | Preparation Time: 5 minutes | Cooking Time: 25 minutes

Ingredients:

- halved mushrooms - 1 pound
- Italian seasoning - 1 tsp.
- olive oil - 3 tbsps.
- tomato sauce with no-salt-added - 1 c.
- yellow onion, chopped - 1

Procedure:

1. Mix the mushrooms with the oil, onion, Italian seasoning and tomato sauce, toss well, and allow to cook for 25 minutes while covered
2. Set in serving plates and enjoy your side dish.

Nutrition per serving:

Calories 96, Fat 7.5g, Cholesterol 1mg, Sodium 219mg, Carbs 6.5g, Fiber 1.8g, Sugars 3.9g, Protein 3.1g, Potassium 403mg

7.15 Honey sage carrots

Serves: 4 | Preparation Time: 27 minutes | Cooking Time: 8 minutes

Ingredients:

- sliced carrots - 2 c.
- ground black pepper - 1/4 tsp.
- butter - 2 tsps.
- honey - 2 tbsps.
- chopped fresh sage - 1 tbsp.
- salt - 1/8 tsp.

Procedure:

1. Load a medium saucepan with water and allow to boil. Mix in carrots and cook for 5 minutes until tender. Drain excess water and place aside.
3. A medium sauté pan is preheated, and butter is added. Add the carrots, sugar, sage, pepper, and salt until the pan is heated and the butter is melting. Sauté for approximately 3 minutes, stirring regularly. Enjoy.

Nutrition per serving:

Calories: 217, Fat: 5g, Fiber: 8g, Sugars 12g, Protein: 4g, sodium: 94mg, potassium: 460 mg

8 POULTRY RECIPES

8.1 Turkey with Spring Onions

Serves: 4 | Preparation Time: 10 minutes | Cooking Time: 30 minutes

Ingredients:

- black peppercorns - ½ tbsp.
- cubed boneless & skinless turkey breast - 1 pound
- water - 1 c.
- chopped spring onions - 2 tbsps.
- cubed tomatoes - 2
- olive oil - 1 tbsp.

Procedure:

1. Using your pan set on a medium high intensity source of heat, pour in oil and heat. Mix in your garlic and cook for about 5 minutes until well browned.
2. Mix in the remaining ingredients and cook while covered for 25 additional minutes.

Nutrition per serving:

167 calories, 20.5g protein, 8.7g carbs, 5.7g fat, 1.8g fiber, 48mg cholesterol, 1188mg sodium, 517mg potassium

8.2 Chicken with Tomatoes and Celery Stalk

Serves: 4 | Preparation Time: 10 minutes | Cooking Time: 40 minutes

Ingredients:

- skinless & boneless chicken breasts, cubed - 2 pounds
- celery stalk, chopped - 1
- cubed tomato - 1
- sliced red onions - 2
- cubed zucchini - 1
- olive oil - 2 tbsps.
- Black pepper – ¼ tsp.
- Water - 1 c.

Procedure:

1. Using a pot, add in all ingredients and mix well.
2. Cook over medium heat for 40 minutes while covered.

Nutrition per serving:

530 calories, 67.2g protein, 8.7g carbs, 24.1g fat, 2.4g fiber, 202mg cholesterol, 234mg sodium, 857mg potassium

8.3 Chicken Bowl with Red Cabbage

Serves: 4 | Preparation Time: 10 minutes | Cooking Time: 25 minutes

Ingredients:

- sweet paprika - 1 tsp.

- skinless & boneless boiled chicken breast, cubed - 1 pound
- carrots, peeled and grated - 2
- low-fat yogurt - 1/3 c.
- red cabbage head, shredded - 1
- black pepper - ½ tsp.

Procedure:

1. Mix chicken and carrots. Place in a bowl.
2. Add sweet paprika, yogurt, cabbage, and ground black pepper.
3. Carefully mix the meal.

Nutrition per serving:

261 calories, 27.1g protein, 16.7g carbs, 10.1g fat, 6.1g fiber, 73mg cholesterol, 130mg sodium, 889mg potassium

8.4 Chicken Sandwich

Serves: 4 | Preparation Time: 10 minutes | Cooking Time: 25 minutes

Ingredients:

- skinless & boneless boiled chicken breast sliced into 4 pieces - 1
- oregano, chopped - 1 tbsp.
- low-fat yogurt - 1 tbsp.
- low-fat cheddar cheese, shredded - ½ c.
- whole-wheat bread slices - 4

Procedure:

1. Mix low-fat yogurt with oregano.
2. Then spread yogurt mixture to the bread slices. Add a topping of sliced chicken breast and Cheddar cheese.
3. Top the sandwich with the rest of your bread slices.

Nutrition per serving:

265 calories, 21.2g protein, 22.1g carbs, 10.6g fat, 6.3g fiber, 47mg cholesterol, 985mg sodium, 572mg potassium

8.5 Turkey and Zucchini Tortillas

Serves: 4 | Preparation Time: 10 minutes | Cooking Time: 20 minutes

Ingredients:

- whole-wheat tortillas - 4
- fat-free yogurt - ½ c.
- boneless & skinless turkey breast cut into strips - 1 pound
- olive oil - 1 tbsp.
- cubed zucchini - 1

Procedure:

1. Mix olive oil, turkey, and zucchini and set in your tray.
2. Bake the ingredients for 20 minutes at 360F.
3. Then place the cooked ingredients on the tortillas and sprinkle with yogurt.

Nutrition per serving:

380 calories, 40.4g protein, 31g carbs, 10.5g fat, 4.9g fiber, 86mg cholesterol, 242mg sodium, 730mg potassium

8.6 Chicken with Eggplants

Serves: 4 | Preparation Time: 10 minutes | Cooking Time: 35 minutes

Ingredients:

- skinless, boneless and cubed chicken breasts - 2
- red onion, chopped - 1
- olive oil - 2 tbsps.
- eggplant, cubed - 1
- smoked paprika - ½ tsp.

Procedure:

1. Mix chicken breast, smoked paprika and olive oil and place in the tray.
2. Add red onion and eggplant.
3. Bake the meal at 360F for 35 minutes.

Nutrition per serving:

524 calories, 25.6g protein, 18.2g carbs, 41.3g fat, 7.7g fiber, 65mg cholesterol, 85mg sodium, 851mg potassium

8.7 Garlic Turkey

Serves: 4 | Preparation Time: 10 minutes | Cooking Time: 40 minutes

Ingredients:

- olive oil - 1 tbsp.
- big boneless, skinless and sliced turkey breast - 1
- minced garlic cloves - 2
- balsamic vinegar - 2 tbsps.

Procedure:

4. Using a baking dish, mix turkey alongside all ingredients and cook at 360F for 40 minutes.

Nutrition per serving:

149 calories, 17.2g protein, 5.2g carbs, 6.2g fat, 0.5g fiber, 45mg cholesterol, 1017mg sodium, 317mg potassium

8.8 Cheddar Turkey

Serves: 4 | Preparation Time: 10 minutes | Cooking Time: 30 minutes

Ingredients:

- boneless, skinless, and sliced turkey breast - 1 pound
- dried basil - ½ tsp.
- ground cumin - ½ tsp.
- olive oil - 2 tbsps.
- fat-free shredded cheddar cheese - 1 c.
- lime juice - 1 tbsp.

Procedure:

1. Mix turkey breast with olive oil, dried basil, cumin, and lime juice.
2. Set on a tray and let bake for 25 minutes.

3. Then top the turkey with Cheddar cheese and continue cooking for additional 5 minutes.

Nutrition per serving:

301 calories, 26.9g protein, 7g carbs, 18.4g fat, 1.2g fiber, 78mg cholesterol, 1330mg sodium, 487mg potassium

8.9 Parsnip and Turkey Bites

Serves: 4 | Preparation Time: 10 minutes | Cooking Time: 40 minutes

Ingredients:

- boneless, skinless and cubed turkey breast - 1 pound
- peeled and cubed parsnips - 2
- avocado oil - 2 tbsps.
- ground cumin - 2 tsps.
- chopped parsley - 1 tbsp.
- water - 1 c.

Procedure:

1. Using a pan set over a medium high source of heat, add in oil and heat. Mix in turkey breast and allow to saute for about 5 minutes.
2. Mix in the other ingredients and let cook over a medium heat intensity for 30 minutes.

Nutrition per serving:

166 calories, 20.6g protein, 13.5g carbs, 3.1g fat, 2.7g fiber, 49mg cholesterol, 1192mg sodium, 542mg potassium

8.10 Nutmeg Chicken with Tender Chickpeas

Serves: 4 | Preparation Time: 10 minutes | Cooking Time: 40 minutes

Ingredients:

- chopped green bell pepper - 1
- canned chickpeas, drained and no-salt-added - 1 c.
- water - 1 c.
- chopped yellow onion - 1
- boneless, skinless and cubed turkey breast - 1 pound
- ground nutmeg - 1 tsp.
- coconut oil - 1 tsp.

Procedure:

1. Using a pan set over a medium high source of heat, add in coconut oil and let heat. Mix in onion, bell pepper, and turkey, and allow to cook for about 10 minutes as you occasionally stir.
2. Mix in the rest of your ingredients. Allow to simmer to about 30 minutes.

Nutrition per serving:

387 calories, 30g protein, 40.6g carbs, 12.3g fat, 10.6g fiber, 49mg cholesterol, 1201mg sodium, 905mg potassium

8.11 Garam Masala Turkey

Serves: 4 | Preparation Time: 10 minutes | Cooking Time: 30 minutes

Ingredients:

- boneless, skinless, and cubed turkey breast - 2 pounds
- green curry paste - 1 tbsp.
- garam masala - 1 tsp.
- olive oil - 2 tbsps.

Procedure:

1. .Mix turkey breast with green curry paste, and garam masala.
2. Then add olive oil and transfer it to the tray.
3. Bake at 365F for 30 minutes.

Nutrition per serving:

224 calories, 19.8g protein, 16.9g carbs, 8.9g fat, 5g fiber, 38mg cholesterol, 941mg sodium, 491mg potassium

8.12 Hot Chicken Mix

Serves: 4 | Preparation Time: 10 minutes | Cooking Time: 30 minutes

Ingredients:

- chopped scallions - 4
- olive oil - 1 tbsp.
- skinless, boneless, and sliced chicken breast - 1 pound
- grated ginger - 1 tbsp.
- dried oregano - 1 tsp.
- ground cumin - 1 tsp.
- chili powder - 1 tsp.

Procedure:

1. Mix chicken breast with all remaining ingredients and place in the tray. .Bake the meal at 360F for 30 minutes.

Nutrition per serving:

180 calories, 25.1g protein, 3.9g carbs, 6.9g fat, 1.6g fiber, 73mg cholesterol, 97mg sodium, 551mg potassium

8.13 Mustard and Garlic Chicken

Serves: 4 | Preparation Time: 10 minutes | Cooking Time: 35 minutes

Ingredients:

- boneless and skinless chicken thighs - 1 pound
- avocado oil - 1 tbsp.
- mustard - 2 tbsps.
- minced garlic cloves - 3
- dried basil - ½ tsp.

Procedure:

1. Mix avocado oil with mustard, garlic, and basil.
2. Then rub the chicken thighs with mustard mixture. Bake for 35 minutes at 365F.

Nutrition per serving:

253 calories, 34.7g protein, 3.3g carbs, 10.5g fat, 1g fiber, 101mg cholesterol, 132mg sodium, 343mg potassium

8.14 Paprika Chicken

Serves: 4 | Preparation Time: 10 minutes | Cooking Time: 25 minutes

Ingredients:

- avocado oil - 1 tbsp.
- boneless, skinless, and cubed chicken breast - 1 pound
- smoked paprika - 1 tbsp.
- onion powder - ¼ tsp.

Procedure:

1. Rub the chicken breast with avocado oil, smoked paprika, and onion powder.
2. Set it in a baking tray and bake at 365F for 25 minutes.

Nutrition per serving:

237 calories, 25.8g protein, 4.5g carbs, 12.9g fat, 1.5g fiber, 73mg cholesterol, 81mg sodium, 652mg potassium

8.15 Chicken with Tomatoes

Serves: 4 | Preparation Time: 10 minutes | Cooking Time: 25 minutes

Ingredients:

- avocado oil - 2 tbsps.
- ground black pepper - 1 tsp.
- skinless, boneless, and cubed chicken breasts - 2
- cherry tomatoes, halved - 1 c.

Procedure:

1. Mix avocado oil chicken breast, and ground black pepper.
2. Place them on the tray, add cherry tomatoes and bake the meal at 365F for 25 minutes.

Nutrition per serving:

38 calories, 2g protein, 6.2g carbs, 1.2g fat, 2.5g fiber, 0mg cholesterol, 8mg sodium, 353mg potassium

8.16 Basil Turkey

Serves: 4 | Preparation Time: 10 minutes | Cooking Time: 25 minutes

Ingredients:

- olive oil - 1 tbsp.
- big boneless, skinless, and cubed turkey breast - 1
- dried basil - 1 tbsp.
- lemon juice - ½ tsp.

Procedure:

3. Mix turkey breast, lemon juice, dried basil, and olive oil.
4. Place the turkey on your tray and set in the oven.
5. Bake at 365F for about 25 minutes.

Nutrition per serving:

121 calories, 2.3g protein, 6.1g carbs, 10.8g fat, 1.9g fiber, 0mg cholesterol, 23mg sodium, 250mg potassium

9 RED MEAT DISHES

9.1 Pork with Cherry Tomatoes

Serves: 4 | Preparation Time: 10 minutes | Cooking Time: 30 minutes

Ingredients:

- avocado oil - 1 tbsp.
- cherry tomatoes, halved - 1 c.
- apple cider vinegar - 2 tbsps.
- pork tenderloin, chopped - 4 oz.

Procedure:

1. Place all ingredients in the tray and gently mix.
2. Cook the meal at 365F for 30 minutes.

Nutrition per serving:

125 calories, 9.1g protein, 6.8g carbs, 6.4g fat, 0.6g fiber, 24mg cholesterol, 49mg sodium, 269mg potassium

9.2 Thyme Pork Skillet

Serves: 4 | Preparation Time: 10 minutes | Cooking Time: 25 minutes

Ingredients:

- pork top loin, boneless, chopped - 1 pound
- olive oil - 1 tbsp.
- chopped yellow onion - 1
- dried thyme - 1 tbsp.
- water - 1 c.
- low-sodium tomato paste - 1 tbsp.

Procedure:

1. Set a pan over a medium high source of heat. Add in oil and heat. Mix in onion and allow to cook for about 5 minutes.
2. Toss in your meat and continue cooking for an additional 5 minutes.
3. Mix in the other ingredients. Continue cooking for additional 15 minutes on medium heat.

Nutrition per serving:

274 calories, 36.6g protein, 5.3g carbs, 11.2g fat, 1.2g fiber, 104mg cholesterol, 104mg sodium, 484mg potassium

9.3 Meat and Zucchini Mix

Serves: 4 | Preparation Time: 10 minutes | Cooking Time: 30 minutes

Ingredients:

- pork top loin boneless, trimmed, and cubed - 2 pounds
- olive oil - 2 tbsps.
- water - ¾ c.
- chopped marjoram - 1 tbsp.
- roughly cubed zucchinis - 2

- sweet paprika - 1 tsp.

Procedure:

1. Place all ingredients in the tray.
2. Gently mix and flatten the ingredients.
3. Cook the meal at 365F for 30 minutes.

Nutrition per serving:

359 calories, 61.1g protein, 5.7g carbs, 9.1g fat, 2.1g fiber, 166mg cholesterol, 166mg sodium, 1289mg potassium

9.4 Garlic Pork

Servings: 4 | Preparation time: 10 minutes | Cooking time: 40 minutes

Ingredients:

- olive oil - 3 tbsps.
- pork rib chop - 2 pounds
- sweet paprika - 2 tsps.
- garlic powder - 1 tsp.

Procedure:

1. Mix garlic powder, sweet paprika and olive oil before rubbing them to the pork rib chops.
2. Place the pork rib chop in the tray and bake at 365F for 40 minutes.

Nutrition per serving:

689 calories, 38.8g protein, 3.2g carbs, 57.1g fat, 1g fiber, 161mg cholesterol, 187mg sodium, 77mg potassium

9.5 Beef with Cauliflower Rice

Serves: 4 | Preparation Time: 10 minutes | Cooking Time: 40 minutes

Ingredients:

- cauliflower rice - 2 c.
- chopped beef top loin - 1 pound
- olive oil - 1 tbsp.
- dried oregano - 1 tsp.
- chopped tomato - 1
- water - ½ c.

Procedure:

1. Mix meat with olive oil, dried oregano, and transfer to the pot.
2. After this, add tomato and cauliflower rice.
3. Then top the ingredients with water and close the pot.
4. Cook the meal at 365f for 40 minutes.

Nutrition per serving:

449calories, 37.3g protein, 38.8g carbs, 14.9g fat, 1.1g fiber, 98mg cholesterol, 137mg sodium, 512mg potassium

9.6 Cilantro Beef Meatballs

Serves: 4 | Preparation Time: 10 minutes | Cooking Time: 30 minutes

Ingredients:

- almond flour - 3 tbsps.
- olive oil - 2 tbsps.

- minced pork tenderloin - 2 pounds

- dried and chopped cilantro - 1 tbsp.

Procedure:

1. Using a mixing bowl, add in cilantro, minced meat and almond flour and mix well.
2. Make the meatballs.
3. Use olive oil to brush the tray.
4. Set the meatballs in your tray. Bake them at 365F for 30 minutes.

Nutrition per serving:

502calories, 67.7g protein, 8.9g carbs, 21.7g fat, 3.6g fiber, 247mg cholesterol, 539mg sodium, 1242mg potassium

9.7 Spiced Meat with Endives

Serves: 4 | Preparation Time: 10 minutes | Cooking Time: 35 minutes

Ingredients:

- chopped pork tenderloin - 1 pound

- water - 1 c.

- trimmed endives (shredded) - 2

- chili powder - 1 tsp.

- ground white pepper - 1 tsp.

- dried oregano - ½ tsp.

- olive oil - 1 tbsp.

Procedure:

1. Mix meat with olive oil, chili powder, white pepper, and dried oregano.
2. Put the meat in the saucepan and roast each side on medium heat for 2 minutes.
3. After this, add water and endives.
4. Simmer for 30 minutes while covered.

Nutrition per serving:

288calories, 34.2g protein, 3.4g carbs, 11.6g fat, 1.2g fiber, 98mg cholesterol, 112mg sodium, 517mg potassium

10 DESSERTS

10.1 Walnut Cake

Serves: 8 | Preparation Time: 10 minutes | Cooking Time: 25 minutes

Ingredients:

- almond flour - 3 c.
- liquid stevia - 5 tbsps.
- chopped walnuts - ½ c.
- baking soda - 2 tsps.
- almond milk - 2 c.
- melted coconut oil - ½ c.

Procedure:

1. Mix almond flour with liquid stevia, almond milk, baking soda, and coconut oil.
2. Stir the mixture to make it smooth before adding walnuts.
3. Stir the mixture well.
4. Then set the cake mixture into your baking mold. Bake until the surface of the cake is light brown for 25 minutes at a heat intensity of 365F.

Nutrition per serving:

464calories, 5.5g protein, 30.6g carbs, 37.8g fat, 3g fiber, 0g cholesterol, 328mg sodium, 201mg potassium

10.2 Vanilla Apple Cake

Serves: 4 | Preparation Time: 10 minutes | Cooking Time: 30 minutes

Ingredients:

- almond milk - 1 c.
- baking powder - 1 tsp.
- vanilla extract - 1 tsp.
- coconut flour - 2 c.
- green apples, sweet, cored, peeled and chopped - 2
- Cooking spray

Procedure:

1. Using a mixing bowl, add in coconut flour, vanilla extract, baking powder, and almond milk and mmix well. Stir the mixture until smooth.
2. After this, add apples and gently mix the mixture one more time.
3. Spray the baking mold with cooking spray from inside.
4. Transfer the apple mixture to the baking mold, flatten it gently, and cook at 365F for 30 minutes.

Nutrition per serving:

305calories, 4.7g protein, 29.8g carbs, 21.5g fat, 5.6g fiber, 0g cholesterol, 347mg sodium, 403mg potassium

10.3 Coconut and Cinnamon Cream

Serves: 4 | Preparation Time: 2 minutes | Cooking Time: 0 minutes

Ingredients:

- coconut cream - 1 c.
- coconut sugar - 2 c.
- cinnamon powder - 2 tbsps.
- coconut shred - 1 tbsp.

Procedure:

5. Using a blender, add in all ingredients, mix well and process for about 30 seconds.

Nutrition per serving:

602calories, 1.6g protein, 125.5g carbs, 14.9g fat, 1.3g fiber, 0g cholesterol, 308mg sodium, 159mg potassium

10.4 Strawberries and Coconut Bowls

Serves: 4 | Preparation Time: 10 minutes | Cooking Time: 0 minutes

Ingredients:

- chopped strawberries - 2 c.
- coconut cream - 1 c.
- coconut shred - ¼ c.

Procedure:

6. Mix coconut cream with coconut shred.
7. Put the coconut mixture in the serving plates. Add a topping of strawberries and enjoy.

Nutrition per serving:

67calories, 2.2g protein, 13g carbs, 0.2g fat, 1.4g fiber, 2g cholesterol, 29mg sodium, 112mg potassium

10.5 Cinnamon Plums

Serves: 4 | Preparation Time: 10 minutes | Cooking Time: 10 minutes

Ingredients:

- halved plums, stones removed - 1 pound
- cinnamon powder - ½ tsp.

Procedure:

8. Use the cinnamon powder to sprinkle over the plums. Set them on your baking tray.
9. Bake for 10 minutes at 365F.

Nutrition per serving:

31calories, 0.2g protein, 8.1g carbs, 0.2g fat, 0.3g fiber, 0g cholesterol, 3mg sodium, 26g potassium

10.6 Baked Apples with Nuts

Serves: 4 | Preparation Time: 10 minutes | Cooking Time: 15 minutes

Ingredients:

- cored and halved green apples - 4
- ground cinnamon - 1 tsp.
- coconut oil - 1 tsp.

- chopped nuts - 2 oz.

Procedure:

1. Put the apples in the tray and sprinkle with ground cinnamon and coconut oil.
2. Then sprinkle the apples with nuts and bake at 365F for 15 minutes.

Nutrition per serving:

156calories, 1.6g protein, 33.4g carbs, 2.3g fat, 5.1g fiber, 0g cholesterol, 15mg sodium, 240g potassium

10.7 Green Tea and Banana Sweetening Mix

Serves: 3-4 | Preparation Time: 10 minutes | Cooking Time: 5 minutes

Ingredients:

- coconut cream - 1 c.
- pitted avocados, chopped - 2 c.
- peeled and chopped bananas - 2
- green tea powder - 2 tbsps.
- palm sugar - 1 tbsp.
- grated lime zest - 2 tbsps.

Procedure:

1. Using an instant pot, add in all the ingredients.
2. Toss this, cover, and then cook for 5 minutes on Low. Perform a manual, natural pressure release, divide and serve it cold.

Nutrition per serving:

Calories: 207, Fat: 2.1g, Carbs: 11.2g, Net Carbs: 8.1g, Protein: 3.1g, Fiber: 8g, Sodium: 154mg, Potassium: 187mg.

10.8 Grapefruit Compote

Serves: 4 | Preparation Time: 5 minutes | Cooking Time: 8 minutes

Ingredients:

- palm sugar - 1 c.
- Sugar-free red grapefruit juice - 64 oz.
- chopped mint - ½ c.
- peeled and cubed grapefruits - 2

Procedure:

3. Take all ingredients and combine them into Instant Pot.
4. Cook for 8 minutes on Low setting, then divide into serving bowls and enjoy!

Nutrition per serving:

Calories: 131, Fat: 1g, Carbs: 12g, Net Carbs: 11g, Protein: 2g, Fiber: 2g, Sodium: 175mg, Potassium: 198mg.

10.9 Instant Pot Applesauce

Serves: 8 | Preparation Time: 10 minutes | Cooking Time: 10 minutes

Ingredients:

- apples - 3 pounds
- water - ½ c.

Procedure:

1. Core and peel the apples and then put them at the bottom of the Instant Pot and then secure the lid. Ensure the vent is sealed before cooking for 10 minutes. Perform a natural pressure release.
2. From there, when it's safe to remove the lid, take the apples and juices and blend this till smooth.
3. Store it in jars or enjoy immediately.

Nutrition per serving:

Calories: 88, Fat: 0g, Carbs: 23g, Net Carbs: 19g, Protein: 0g, Fiber: 4g, Sodium: 186mg, Potassium: 321mg.

10.10 Rice and Fruits Pudding

Serves: 4 | Preparation Time: 10 minutes | Cooking Time: 25 minutes

Ingredients:

- cooked black rice - 1 c.
- cored and cubed pears - 2
- cinnamon powder - 2 tsps.
- coconut milk - ½ c.

Procedure:

1. Using a mixing bowl, add in all ingredients and mix well. Set to your baking ramekins.
2. Bake the pudding for 25 minutes at 350F.

Nutrition per serving:

341 calories, 2.3g protein, 85.2g carbs, 0.9g fat, 3.8g fiber, 0g cholesterol, 13mg sodium, 192g potassium

10.11 Rhubarb and Pear Compote

Serves: 4 | Preparation Time: 10 minutes | Cooking Time: 15 minutes

Ingredients:

- roughly chopped rhubarb - 2 c.
- chopped pears - 2
- water - 2 c.

Procedure:

1. Using a pot, add in all ingredients. Heat until the mixture boils.
2. Simmer the compote for 15 minutes.
3. Cool the compote well before serving.

Nutrition per serving:

53calories, 0.7g protein, 11.8g carbs, 0.2g fat, 1.1g fiber, 0g cholesterol, 6mg sodium, 178g potassium

10.12 Lime Cake

Serves: 6 | Preparation Time: 10 minutes | Cooking Time: 35 minutes

Ingredients:

- whole wheat flour - 2 c.
- melted coconut oil - 2 tbsps.
- whisked egg - 1

- baking powder - 1 tsp.
- coconut milk - 1 c.
- sliced lemon - ½

Procedure:

1. Mix flour with baking powder, coconut oil, egg, and coconut milk.
2. When the mixture is homogenous, transfer it to the baking pan.
3. 3.Top the cake with lemon slices and bake at 360F for 35 minutes.

Nutrition per serving:

324calories, 6.2g protein, 42.3g carbs, 15.3g fat, 2.1g fiber, 27g cholesterol, 35mg sodium, 252g potassium

10.13 Coconut Shred Bars

Serves: 6 | Preparation Time: 10 minutes | Cooking Time: 25 minutes

Ingredients:

- coconut flour - 2 c.
- baking powder - 1 tsp.
- nutmeg (ground) - ½ tsp.
- melted coconut oil - 1 c.
- coconut shred - 1 c.
- whisked egg - 1

Procedure:

1. Add all the above ingredients into your bowl and mix until smooth.
2. Set the mixture in your baking tray, gently flatten and bake at a heat intensity of 380 F for 25 minutes. Slice the bars and enjoy cold.

Nutrition per serving:

579calories, 3.7g protein, 53.7g carbs, 41.9g fat, 2g fiber, 27g cholesterol, 17mg sodium, 275g potassium

10.14 Cocoa Squares

Serves: 4 | Preparation Time: 10 minutes | Cooking Time: 20 minutes

Ingredients:

- chopped peaches - 3
- baking soda - ½ tsp.
- coconut flour - 1 c.
- melted coconut oil - 4 tbsps.
- cocoa powder - 2 tbsps.

Procedure:

1. Blend the peaches with all remaining ingredients to obtain a smooth mixture.
2. Using a lined square pan, pour in the mixture, spread well before baking in your oven for 20 minutes at 375 F.

3.When the dessert is cool, cut it into squares.

Nutrition per serving:

221calories, 3.1g protein, 17.2g carbs, 17.8g fat, 3.4g fiber, 0g cholesterol, 162mg sodium, 282g potassium

11 SMOOTHIES RECIPES

11.1 Blueberry-Vanilla Yogurt Smoothie

Serves: 2 | Preparation Time: 5 minutes | Cooking Tim: 0 minutes

Ingredients:

- blueberries (frozen) - 1½ c.
- nonfat vanilla Greek yogurt - 1 c.
- nonfat or low-fat milk - 1 c.
- frozen and peeled banana, sliced - 1
- ice - 1 c.

Procedure:

1. Using a mixer, add in all ingredients. Blend well until you have a creamy and smooth consistency.
2. Enjoy immediately.

Nutrition per serving:

Calories: 228, Fat: 1g, Sodium: 63mg, Potassium: 470mg, Carbs: 45g, Fiber: 5g, Sugars: 34g, Protein: 12g

11.2 Peaches And Greens Smoothie

Serves : 2 | Preparation Time: 5 minutes | Cooking Time: 0

Ingredients:

- fresh spinach - 2 c.
- frozen peaches (or fresh, pitted) - 1 c.
- ice - 1 c.
- low-fat or nonfat milk - ½ c.
- plain nonfat or low-fat Greek yogurt - ½ c.
- vanilla extract - ½ tsp.
- Optional: no-calorie sweetener of choice

Procedure:

1. Add all of the components to a mixer and process until smooth.
2. Enjoy immediately.

Nutrition per serving:

Calories: 191; Total Fat: 0g; Saturated Fat: 0g; Cholesterol: 7mg; Sodium: 157mg; Potassium: 984mg; Total Carbs: 30g; Fiber: 3g; Sugars: 23g; Protein: 18g

11.3 Banana Breakfast Smoothie

Serves: 1 | Preparation Time: 10 minutes | Cooking Time: 5 minutes

Ingredients:

- frozen banana - 1
- 1% low-fat milk - ½ c.
- Honey - 1 tbsp.
- vanilla yogurt, fat-free - 1 (6 oz.) carton

- crushed ice - ½ c.

Procedure:

1. Add all the above ingredients into your blender.
2. Pulse it until smooth and creamy on high setting.
3. Set in a glass to serve.

Nutrition per serving:

Calories 82, Carbs: 3.1 g, Protein: 4 g, Fat: 0.2 g, Saturated fat: 0g, Cholesterol: 0 mg, Sodium: 11 mg, Fiber: 2.4 g, Sugar: 4.3 g, Calcium: 111 mg,| Potassium: 659mg

11.4 Chocolate Berry Smoothie

Serves: 1 | Preparation Time: 10 minutes| Cooking Time: 5 minutes

Ingredients:

- cold water - 1 ½ c.
- Frozen blueberries - ¼ c.
- avocado - ½
- Cashews - 2 tbsps.
- Organic cocoa powder - 2 tbsps.
- Vanilla extract - ½ tsp.

Procedure:

1. Add all the above ingredients into your blender.
2. Pulse on high setting until the mixture becomes smooth and creamy.
3. Pour in a glass and enjoy it.

Nutrition per serving:

Calories 251, Total Fat 17.1 g, Fiber 7.8 g , Protein 6.5 g, Sugar 8.1 g, Sodium 56 mg , Potassium: 1412mg

11.5 Tropical Turmeric Smoothie

Serves: 1 | Preparation Time: 10 minutes | Cooking Time: 5 minutes

Ingredients:

- turmeric - ½ tsp.
- Almond milk - 1 c.
- ginger - ½ tsp.
- banana - 1
- Olive oil - 1 tbsp.
- frozen mango - ½ c.
- cinnamon - ½ tsp.

Procedure:

1. Using your blender, mix in the above ingredients.
2. Pulse it using high speed setting until the mixture becomes smooth and creamy.
3. Set in a glass and serve.

Nutrition per serving:

Calories 143,Total Fat 4.5 g, Fiber 3.4 g, Protein 3.3 g, Sugar 11 g, Sodium 21 mg, Potassium: 962mg

11.6 Carrot Juice Smoothie

Serves: 1| Preparation Time: 10 minutes | Cooking Time: 5 minutes

Ingredients:

- almond milk (unsweetened) - 1 c.
- ripe banana - 1
- cinnamon - ½ tsp.
- fresh ginger - ½ tbsp.
- carrot juice - ½ c.
- frozen pineapple - 1 c.
- Ground turmeric - ¼ tsp.
- Lime juice - 1 tbsp.

Procedure:

1. Using your blender, add in and mix the above ingredients.
2. Pulse using high speed until the mixture becomes smooth and creamy.
3. Serve in a glass.

Nutrition per serving:

Calories: 143, Fat: 2.4g, Carbs: 31g, Sugar: 17.4g, Sodium: 113mg, Fiber: 4g, Protein: 2.3g, Potassium: 697mg

11.7 Mixed Berries Smoothie

Serves: 2 | Preparation Time: 4 minutes | Cooking Time: 0 minutes

Ingredients:

- frozen blueberries - ¼ c.
- frozen blackberries - ¼ c.
- almond milk (unsweetened) - 1 c.
- vanilla bean extract - 1 tsp.
- flaxseeds - 3 tsps.
- chilled Greek yogurt - 1 scoop
- Stevia as needed

Procedure:

1. Mix everything in a blender and emulsify.
2. Pulse the mixture four time until you have your desired thickness.
3. Serve in a glass.

Nutrition per serving:

Calories: 221,Fat: 9g, Protein: 21g, Carbs: 10g, Sodium: 78 mg

11.8 Satisfying Berry and Almond Smoothie

Serves: 4 | Preparation Time: 10 minutes | Cooking Time: 0 minutes

Ingredients:

- whole banana - 1
- blueberries (frozen) - 1 c.
- almond butter - 1 tbsp.
- almond milk - ½ c.
- Water, enough as required

Procedure:

1. Add the listed ingredients to your blender and blend well until you have a smoothie-like texture.
2. Chill and serve.

3. Enjoy!

Nutrition per serving:

Calories: 321, Fat: 11g, Carbs: 55g, Protein: 5g, Sodium: 46 mg

11.9 Refreshing Mango and Pear Smoothie

Serves: 1 | Preparation Time: 10 minutes | Cooking Time: 0 minutes

Ingredients:

- chopped ripe mango, cored - 1
- mango, peeled, pitted and chopped - ½
- chopped kale - 1 c.
- plain Greek yogurt - ½ c.
- ice cubes - 2

Procedure:

1. Add pear, mango, yogurt, kale, and mango to a blender and puree.
2. Add ice and blend well to obtain a mixture with a smooth texture.
3. Enjoy!

Nutrition per serving:

Calories: 293, Fat: 8g, Carbs: 53g, Protein: 8g, Sodium: 36 mg

11.10 Blackberry and Apple Smoothie

Serves: 2 | Preparation Time: 5 minutes | Cooking Time: 20 minutes

Ingredients:

- frozen blackberries - 2 c.
- apple cider - ½ c.
- cubed apple, - 1
- non-fat lemon yogurt - 2/3 c.

Procedure:

1. In a blender, add the above ingredients. Thoroughly blend well to obtain a smooth consistency.
2. Chill before serving.

Nutrition per serving:

Calories: 200, Fat: 10g, Carbs: 14g, Protein 2g, Sodium: 42mg

11.11 Raspberry Green Smoothie

Serves: 1 | Preparation Time: 10 minutes | Cooking Time: 10 minutes

Ingredients:

- Raspberries – 1 c.
- Water – 1 c.
- spinach - ¼ c.
- Chia seeds - 1 tbsp.
- Lemon juice - 2 tbsps.
- banana - 1
- Almond butter - 1 tbsp.

Procedure:

1. .Using a blender, add in all ingredients. Pulse well to get a creamy and smooth consistency.

2. Set in a glass and enjoy.

Nutrition per serving:

Calories: 176, Fat: 2.1 g, Carbs: 6.7 g, Sugar: 11.5 g, Sodium: 45 mg, Fiber: 7.6 g, Protein: 3.4 g, Potassium: 534mg

11.12 Blueberry Smoothie

Serves: 2 | Preparation Time: 10 minutes | Cooking Time: 5 minutes

Ingredients:

- spinach - 1 c.
- pineapple - 2 c.
- coconut water - 4 c.
- blueberries - 1 c.
- apple - 1
- watermelon - 2 c.

Procedure:

1. Using your blender, add in ingredients.
2. Pulse on high setting until you obtain a creamy and smooth consistency.
3. Set in a glass to enjoy.

Nutrition per serving:

Calories: 213, Fat: 4.3 g, Carbs: 10.4 g, Sugar: 17 g, Sodium: 48 mg, Fiber: 7.9 g, Protein: 5 g, Potassium: 1817mg

11.13 Avocado Smoothie

Serves: 1 | Preparation Time: 10 minutes | Cooking Time: 5 minutes

Ingredients:

- Cacao powder - 2 tbsps.
- Avocado - ½
- frozen banana - ½
- Chia seeds - ½ tsp.
- Plain almond milk - ¼ c.
- Lime juice (optional) - 2 tbsps.

Procedure:

1. With the use of your blender, add the above ingredients. Process on high speed to get a creamy and smooth consistency.
2. Enjoy.

Nutrition per serving:

Calories: 234, Fat: 4.4 g, Carbs: 12.3 g, Sugar: 16.4 g, Sodium: 53 mg, Fiber: 8.4 g, Protein: 5.6 g, Potassium: 1618mg

11.14 Chocolate and Peanut Butter Smoothie

Serves: 4 | Preparation Time: 5 minutes | Cooking Time: 0 minutes

Ingredients:

- unsweetened cocoa powder - 1 tbsp.
- peanut butter - 1 tbsp.
- banana - 1
- maca powder - 1 tsp.
- unsweetened soy milk - ½ c.

- rolled oats - ¼ c.
- flaxseeds - 1 tbsp.
- maple syrup - 1 tbsp.
- water - 1 c.

Procedure:

1. Add in the above ingredients to your blender, then process until creamy and smooth consistency is achieved. Add water or soy milk if necessary.
2. Serve.

Nutrition per serving:

Calories: 474, Fat: 16.0g, Carbs: 27.0g, Fiber: 18.0g, Protein: 13.0g, Sodium: 53mg, Potassium: 89mg.

11.15 Ultimate Fruit Smoothie

Serves: 1 | Preparation Time: 10 minutes | Cooking Time: 10 minutes

Ingredients:

- strawberries - 2
- 2% milk - ½ c.
- mango, cut into chunks - ½
- fresh peach sliced - ½
- orange juice - ½ c.
- pineapple - ¼ c.

Procedure:

1. Using a blender, mix in strawberries, milk, mango chunks, peach slices, orange juice and pineapple.
2. Blend well until smooth.
3. Add more milk if required.
4. Serve

Nutrition per serving:

225 calories, protein 5.8g, carbs 46.4g, fat 3.1g, cholesterol 9.8mg, sodium 35.9mg, Potassium: 1329mg

11.16 Oat Cocoa Smoothie

Serves: 1 | Preparation Time: 10 minutes | Cooking Time: 5 minutes

Ingredients:

- vanilla extract - 1 tsp.
- Skim milk - ¾ c.
- plain low-fat yogurt - ½ c.
- Ground flaxseed - 1 tbsp.
- banana - 1
- Unsweetened cocoa powder - 1 tbsp.
- Quick-cook oats - ¼ c.
- ground cinnamon - a dash

Procedure:

1. Place all ingredients in your blender. Process well to obtain a smooth consistency. Add more milk if required.
2. Enjoy.

Nutrition per serving:

350 calories, 19 g protein, 5 g fat, 1 g saturated fat, 60 g carbs, 7 g fiber, 6 mg cholesterol, 177 mg sodium, 1381mg potassium

11.17 Tropical Green Breakfast Smoothie

Serves: 2 | Preparation Time: 10 minutes | Cooking Time: 5 minutes

Ingredients:

- banana cut in chunks - 1
- baby spinach - 1 c.
- plain Greek yogurt - 1/4 c.
- Pineapple chunks - 1 c.
- Pineapple juice or water - ¼ c.
- oats - 1/3 c.
- mango cut in chunks 1

Procedure:

1. Place all ingredients in your blender. Process well to obtain a smooth consistency.
2. Enjoy.

Nutrition per serving:
265 calories, protein 6 g, carbs 32.3 g, fat 3.4 g, cholesterol 7.5 mg, sodium 21.4 mg, potassium: 532mg

11.18 Green Apple Smoothie

Serves: 2 | Preparation Time: 10 minutes | Cooking Time: 5 minutes

Ingredients:

- Apple cider - 1 c.
- banana - 1
- Kale, stems removed - 2 c.
- cinnamon – a pinch
- Green apple cut into chunks - 1 c.
- Water or ice - 1 c.

Procedure:

1. Place all ingredients in your blender. Process well to obtain a smooth consistency.
2. Enjoy.

Nutrition per serving:

Calories 233, Total Fat 0.5g, Sodium 31.7mg, Total Carbs 56.4g, Dietary Fiber 3.6g, sugars 30.8g, Protein 2g, Potassium: 479mg

12 SNACKS RECIPES

12.1 Corn and Cayenne Pepper Spread

Serves: 4 | Preparation Time: 30 minutes | Cooking Time: 0 minutes

Ingredients:

- cayenne pepper - ½ tsp.
- boiled corn - 2 c.
- non-fat cream cheese - 1 c.

Procedure:

1. In the bowl, put all ingredients from the list above.
2. Carefully mix the spread.

Nutrition per serving:

215 calories, 4g protein, 18.4g carbs, 16.2g fat, 3.8g fiber, 0mg cholesterol, 22mg sodium, 397mg potassium

12.2 Black Beans Bars

Serves: 12 | Preparation Time: 2 hours | Cooking Time: 0 minutes

Ingredients:

- no-salt-added canned and drained black beans - 1 c.
- chia seeds - ½ c.
- coconut cream - 1 tbsp.

Procedure:

1. 1.Blend the black beans until smooth.
2. 2.After this, mix them with chia seeds and coconut cream.
3. 3.Make the bars from the mixture and store them in the fridge.

Nutrition per serving:

calories, 6.4g protein, 16.9g carbs, 8g fat, 6.5g fiber, 1mg cholesterol, 19mg sodium, 328mg potassium

12.3 Pepper and Chickpeas Hummus

Serves: 4 | Preparation Time: 10 minutes | Cooking Time: 0 minutes

Ingredients:

- no-salt-added canned chickpeas, drained and rinsed - 14 oz.
- sesame paste - 1 tbsp.
- roasted chopped red peppers - 2
- Juice of ½ lemon
- chopped walnuts - 4

Procedure:

1. In your blender, combine the chickpeas with the sesame paste, red peppers, lemon juice and walnuts, pulse properly, divide in serving bowls. Enjoy your snack.
2. Enjoy!

Nutrition per serving:

calories 231, fat 12, fiber 6, carbs 15, protein 14, sodium 300mg, potassium 714mg

12.4 Lemony Chickpeas Dip

Serves: 4 | Preparation Time: 10 minutes | Cooking Time: 0 minutes

Ingredients:

- no-salt-added canned chickpeas, drained, rinsed - 14 oz.
- grated zest of 1 lemon
- Juice of 1 lemon
- olive oil - 1 tbsp.
- pine nuts - 4 tbsps.
- chopped coriander - ½ c.

Procedure:

1. Using a blender, pulse lemon juice, oil, lemon zest, coriander and chickpeas.
2. Set in serving bowls and top with sprinkles of pine nuts before enjoying.

Nutrition per serving:

calories 200, fat 12g, fiber 4g, carbs 9g, protein 7g, sodium 212mg, potassium 544mg

12.5 Red Pepper Muffins with Mozzarella

Serves: 12 | Preparation Time: 10 minutes | Cooking Time: 30 minutes

Ingredients:

- flour (whole wheat) - 1 ¾ c.
- coconut sugar - 2 tbsps.
- baking powder - 2 tsps.
- black pepper - A pinch
- egg - 1
- almond milk - ¾ c.
- roasted and chopped red pepper - 2/3 c.
- low-fat shredded mozzarella - ½ c.

Procedure:

1. Using a bowl, combine coconut sugar, flour, baking powder, black pepper, egg, milk, red pepper and mozzarella, stir well, divide into a lined muffin tray, place in your oven. Set to bake for 30 minutes at a heat intensity of 400°F.
2. Enjoy!

Nutrition per serving:

calories 149, fat 4, fiber 2, carbs 14, protein 5 sodium 64mg, potassium 474mg

12.6 Nuts And Seeds Mix

Serves: 6 | Preparation Time: 10 minutes | Cooking Time: 0 minutes

Ingredients:

- pecans - 1 c.
- hazelnuts - 1 c.

- almonds - 1 c.
- shredded coconut - ¼ c.
- walnuts - 1 c.
- dried papaya pieces - ½ c.
- dates, dried, pitted and chopped - ½ c.
- sunflower seeds - ½ c.
- pumpkin seeds - ½ c.
- raisins - 1 c.

Procedure:

1. Using a bowl, mix the coconut, pecans, hazelnuts, almonds, walnuts, papaya, dates, sunflower seeds, pumpkin seeds and raisins, toss and enjoy as a snack.
2. Enjoy!

Nutrition per serving:

Calories 188, fat 4, fiber 6, carbs 8, protein 6, sodium 39mg, potassium 575mg

12.7 Tortilla Chips with Chili

Serves: 6 | Preparation Time: 10 minutes | Cooking Time: 20 minutes

Ingredients:

- whole wheat tortillas, each cut into 6 wedges - 12
- olive oil - 2 tbsps.
- chili powder - 1 tbsp.
- cayenne pepper - A pinch

Procedure:

1. Line your baking sheet using an aluminum foil. Spread over the tortillas, add cayenne, oil, and chili powder. Toss well and set in your oven to ensure you bake for 20 minutes at 350 degrees F.
2. Enjoy as a dish.

Nutrition per serving:

Calories 199, fat 3, fiber 4, carbs 12, protein 5, sodium 266mg, potassium 549mg

12.8 Kale Chips

Serves: 8 | Preparation Time: 10 minutes | Cooking Time: 15 minutes

Ingredients:

- kale leaves - 1 bunch
- olive oil - 1 tbsp.
- smoked paprika - 1 tsp.
- black pepper - A pinch

Procedure:

1. On a baking sheet, spread kale leaves. Add oil, paprika, and black pepper. Toss well before setting in your oven to bake for 15 minutes at 350 degrees F.
2. Set into bowls and enjoy your snack.

Nutrition per serving:

Calories 177, fat 2, fiber 4, carbs 13, protein 6, sodium 15mg, potassium 436mg

12.9 Hearty Buttery Walnuts

Serves: 4 | Preparation Time: 10 minutes | Cooking Time: 0 minutes

Ingredients:

- walnut halves - 4
- almond butter - ½ tbsp.

Procedure:

3. Spread butter over two walnut halves. Top with other halves.
4. Enjoy!

Nutrition per serving:

Calories: 90, Fat: 10g, Carbs: 0g, Protein: 1g, Sodium: 1 mg, Potassium: 440mg

12.10 Spiced Walnuts

Serves: 4 | Preparation Time: 10 minutes | Cooking Time: 15 minutes

Ingredients:

- walnuts - 2 c.
- red vinegar - 3 tbsps.
- olive oil - A drizzle
- cayenne pepper - A pinch

Procedure:

1. Using a mixing bowl, mix walnuts, red vinegar, olive oil, and cayenne pepper.
2. Set the walnuts to a baking tray. Allow to bake for about 15 minutes at 365°F. Stir occasionally to ensure no burning.

Nutrition per serving:

388 calories, 15g protein, 6.2g carbs, 36.9g fat, 4.3g fiber, 0mg cholesterol, 2mg sodium, 331mg potassium

12.11 Radish Chips

Serves: 4 | Preparation Time: 10 minutes | Cooking Time: 20 minutes

Ingredients:

- thinly sliced radishes - 1 pound
- olive oil - 2 tbsps.

Procedure:

1. Mix radish slices with olive oil and transfer them to a baking tray.
2. You then bake the chips for approx. 20 minutes at 365F. Toss the radish from time to time to avoid burning.

Nutrition per serving:

78 calories, 0.8g protein, 3.9g carbs, 7.1g fat, 1.8g fiber, 0mg cholesterol, 44mg sodium, 266mg potassium

12.12 Aromatic Avocado Fries

Serves: 4 | Preparation Time: 5 minutes | Cooking Time: 10 minutes

Ingredients:

- peeled and pitted avocados cut into wedges - 2
- avocado oil - 1 tbsp.
- ground cardamom - 1 tsp.

Procedure:

1. Sprinkle the avocado wedges with avocado oil and cardamom.
2. After this, line a baking paper to a baking tray and arrange avocado wedges inside your tray one by one.
3. Bake the fried for 10 minutes at 375F. Flip to cook the other side after 5 minutes.

Nutrition per serving:

236 calories, 1.9g protein, 6.3g carbs, 8.6g fat, 23.1g fiber, 0mg cholesterol, 6mg sodium, 488mg potassium

12.13 Carrot Chips

Serves: 4 | Preparation Time: 10 minutes | Cooking Time: 30 minutes

Ingredients:

- thinly sliced carrots - 4
- avocado oil - 2 tbsps.
- chili flakes - 1 tsp.
- turmeric powder - ½ tsp.

Procedure:

1. Mix carrot with avocado oil, chili flakes, and turmeric powder.
2. Set the chips on your lined baking sheet. You should bake at 400F for approximately 25 minutes, and flip after 10 minutes to cook the other side.

Nutrition per serving:

88 calories, 0.6g protein, 6.5g carbs, 7.1g fat, 1.8g fiber, 0mg cholesterol, 42mg sodium, 214mg potassium

12.14 Minty Tapenade

Serves: 4 | Preparation Time: 4 minutes | Cooking Time: 0 minutes

Ingredients:

- pitted black olives, chopped - 2 c.
- chopped mint - 1 c.
- avocado oil - 2 tbsps.
- coconut cream - ½ c.

Procedure:

1. Using your blender, add in the above ingredients and carefully blend.

Nutrition per serving:

166 calories, 2.1g protein, 8.2g carbs, 15.4g fat, 4.7g fiber, 0mg cholesterol, 598mg sodium, 211mg potassium

12.15 Nutritious Snack Bowls

Serves: 4 | Preparation Time: 10 minutes | Cooking Time: 20 minutes

Ingredients:

- sunflower seeds - 1 c.
- chia seeds - 1 c.
- water - 1 c.
- cored apples cut into wedges - 2

- ground cardamom - ¼ tsp.

Procedure:

1. Mix water, chia seeds and ground nutmeg and stir gently.
2. Leave the mixture for 20 minutes.
3. After this, mix cooked chia seeds with sunflower seeds, and apples, and gently mix.

Nutrition per serving:

291 calories, 6.3g protein, 27.1g carbs, 19.8g fat, 11.2g fiber, 0mg cholesterol, 6mg sodium, 297mg potassium

12.16 Potato Chips

Serves: 4 | Preparation Time: 10 minutes | Cooking Time: 20 minutes

Ingredients:

- peeled gold potatoes, thinly sliced - 4
- garlic powder - ¼ tsp.
- olive oil - 2 tbsps.
- sweet paprika - 1 tsp.

Procedure:

1. Line a baking paper to a baking sheet. Spread over with sliced potato, add the other ingredients. Gently mix and flatten.
2. Bake the chips for 20 minutes at 390F. Flip after 10 minutes to cook the other side.

Nutrition per serving:

118 calories, 1.3g protein, 13.4g carbs, 7.4g fat, 2.9g fiber, 0mg cholesterol, 19mg sodium, 361mg potassium

12.17 Hot Walnuts

Serves: 8 | Preparation Time: 5 minutes | Cooking Time: 15 minutes

Ingredients:

- smoked paprika - ½ tsp.
- chili powder - ½ tsp.
- garlic powder - ½ tsp.
- avocado oil - 1 tbsp.
- walnuts - 14 oz.

Procedure:

1. Mix walnuts with smoked paprika, and all other ingredients.
2. After this, place the walnuts in your baking tray before flattening well.
3. Allow to bake at 355°F for 15 minutes. Stir them from time to time.

Nutrition per serving:

310 calories, 12g protein, 5.3g carbs, 29.5g fat, 3.6g fiber, 0mg cholesterol, 3mg sodium, 273mg potassium

12.18 Cranberry Crackers

Serves: 4 | Preparation Time: 3 hours 5 minutes | Cooking Time: 0 minutes

Ingredients:

- vanilla extract - ¼ tsp.
- rolled oats - 2 tbsps.
- shredded coconut - 2 tbsps.
- cranberries - 1 c.

Procedure:

1. Put the cranberries in the blender.
2. Add rolled oats, vanilla extract, and shredded coconut.
3. Blend the mixture well.
4. Pour into the baking dish. Bake for 25 minutes or until a skewer inserted in the center comes out clean.
5. Cool on a rack before wrapping in cling film and freezing for at least 2 hours and up to 3 months.
6. Allow the loaf to defrost slightly for 15 minutes so that the exterior is not rock hard frozen.
7. Preheat your oven to 250°F. Put one shelf in the center and another beneath it.
8. Slice the biscuits thinly with a serrated bread knife and place them on two big baking pans; you can cram them in since they won't expand or stick.
9. Bake for 50 minutes, or until light golden, switching pans halfway.
10. Allow the biscuits to cool on the tray; they will stiffen and shatter when broken.

Nutrition per serving:

66 calories, 0.8g protein, 5.4g carbs, 4.4g fat, 1.8g fiber, 0mg cholesterol, 3mg sodium, 102mg potassium

13 SAUCES AND DRESSING RECIPES

13.1 Salsa Verde

Serves: 5 | Preparation Time: 10 minutes | Cooking Time: 5 minutes

Ingredients:

- fresh finely chopped cilantro - 4 tbsps.
- fresh finely chopped parsley - 1/4 c.
- grated garlic cloves - 2
- lemon juice - 2 tsps.
- olive oil - 3/4 c.
- capers - 2 tbsps.
- black pepper - 1/2 tsp.

Procedure:

1. Add the above ingredients to a bowl. It can be mixed by hand or with an immersion blender. Mix until desired consistency is achieved.
2. You can serve over burgers, sandwiches, salads and more. One is allowed to refrigerate for a maximum of 5 days or for longer once you place in a freezer.

Nutrition per serving:

Total Fat: 25.3g, Cholesterol: 0mg, Sodium: 475mg, Protein: 0.2g, Potassium 151mg.

13.2 Caramel Sauce

Serves: 8 | Preparation Time: 10 minutes | Cooking Time: 35 minutes

Ingredients:

- raw cashews - 1/2 c.
- melted coconut cream - 1/2 c.
- liquid stevia - 10 drops
- vegan butter - 2 tbsps.
- vanilla extract - 3 tsps.

Procedure:

1. Preheat your oven to attain 325 degrees F.
2. Place nuts on a greased baking tray and toast until crunchy and lightly golden for 20 minutes.
3. Let the nuts cool slightly and add them to your food processor. Blend to obtain a slightly lumpy consistency.
4. Mix in the rest of your ingredients and blend well until you achieve a smooth and creamy consistency. Do not over blend or the coconut cream will become separated from the rest of the ingredients
5. If not using immediately, refrigerate in an airtight container. To reheat the caramel to make it more flow able, add to a saucepan and gently warm on low heat. It can be served with your favorite

keto vegan treats, such as ice cream.

Nutrition per serving:

Total Fat: 9.8g, Cholesterol: 0mg, Sodium: 29mg, Total carbs: 4.6g, Sodium: 103mg, Potassium: 161mg.

13.3 Authentic Greek Tzatziki Sauce

Serves: makes 1½ cups | Preparation Time: 10 minutes | Cooking Time: 0

Ingredients:

- plain Greek yogurt - 1 c.
- Persian cucumbers - 2
- extra-virgin olive oil - 1 tbsp.
- chopped fresh dill - 2 tbsps.
- freshly chopped mint - 2 tbsps.
- minced garlic clove - 1
- lemon juice - 2 tbsps.
- kosher salt - ½ tsp.

Procedure:

1. Using a box grater to grate the cucumbers.
2. In a medium bowl, mix the lemon juice, grated cucumbers, yogurt, dill, mint, olive oil, garlic, and salt.

Nutrition per serving:

Calories: 45, Total fat: 0g, Saturated fat: 0g, Cholesterol: 0mg, Sodium: 105mg, Potassium: 125mg, Total Carbs: 3g, Fiber: 0g, Sugars: 2g, Protein: 3g, Magnesium: 10mg, Calcium: 45mg

13.4 Beef Taco Filling

Serves: 4 | Preparation Time: 10 minutes | Cooking Time: 20 minutes

Ingredients:

- ground extra lean sirloin, 95% lean - 1 pound (454 g)
- medium taco sauce - ½ bottle
- diced green peppers (fresh or frozen) - 1 c.
- diced onions (fresh or frozen) - 1 c.

Procedure:

1. Using a nonstick skillet, add in beef and heat over a medium-high source of heat. Cook for about 3 minutes before reducing heat to medium intensity. Put in onions and peppers. Proceed to cook for 5 or more minutes, or until thoroughly browned.
2. Add taco sauce, reduce your heat intensity and let simmer for 10 minutes.

Nutrition per serving:

Calories: 140, Protein: 17 g, Carbs: 7 g, Fat: 4 g, Cholesterol: 48 mg, Fiber: 1 g, Sodium: 164 mg, Potassium: 344 mg

13.5 Creamy Avocado Alfredo Sauce

Serves: 4 | Preparation Time: 10 minutes | Cooking Time: 2 minutes

Ingredient:

- peeled and pitted ripe avocado - 1
- olive oil - 1 tbsp.
- dried basil - 1 tbsp.
- clove garlic - 1
- lemon juice - 1 tbsp.
- salt - ⅛ tsp.

Procedure:

1. Add in above ingredients in your food processor. Blend well to get a smooth and creamy sauce.
2. Pour over vegetable noodles and enjoy.

Nutrition per serving:

Calories: 104, Total Fat: 10g, Saturated Fat: 1g, Cholesterol: 0mg, Sodium: 43mg, Potassium: 229mg, Total Carbs: 4g, Fiber: 3g, Sugars: 0g, Protein: 1g

13.6 Vegan Ranch Dressing

Serves: 3 | Preparation Time: 5 minutes | Cooking Time: 10 minutes

Ingredients:

- vegan mayo - 1 c.
- coconut milk - 1 1/2 c.
- scallions - 2
- peeled garlic cloves - 2
- fresh dill - 1 c.
- garlic powder - 1 tsp.
- pepper - ¼ tsp.

Procedure:

1. Add scallion, fresh dill and garlic cloves to your food processor. Pulse well to ensure finely chopped.
2. Mix in the remaining ingredients and continue blending to obtain a smooth and creamy consistency. Makes a great creamy salad dressing. Store in the refrigerator.

Nutrition per serving:

Total Fat: 11.9g, Cholesterol: 0mg, Sodium: 50mg, Fiber: 4g, Potassium 187mg.

13.7 Easy Quick Tangy Barbecue Sauce

Serves: 1½ cups | Preparation Time: 6 minutes | Cooking Time: 1 min

Ingredients:

- no-salt tomato paste - 1 (8 oz.) can
- apple cider vinegar - 1½ tbsps.
- Dijon mustard - 2 tbsps.
- onion powder - 1 tsp.
- molasses - 2 tsps.
- soy sauce (low-sodium) - 1 tbsp.
- garlic powder - 1 tsp.

Procedure:

1. Add the garlic powder, tomato paste, soy sauce, vinegar, Dijon mustard, molasses, and onion powder in a medium bowl and mix well.
2. Pour it in an airtight container and refrigerate for a maximum week.

Nutrition per serving:

Calories: 32, Total Fat: 0g, Saturated Fat: 0g, Protein: 2g, Total Carbs: 7g, Fiber: 1g, Sugars: 4g, Cholesterol: 0mg, Sodium: 240mg, Potassium: 340mg

13.8 Fresh Tomato Basil Sauce

Serves: 6 | Preparation Time: 5 minutes | Cooking Time: 10 minutes

Ingredients:

- olive oil - 2 tbsps.
- no-salt, crushed, or chopped tomatoes - 4 (15 oz.) cans
- finely chopped garlic cloves - 3
- dried basil - 1 tbsp.
- Salt - ¼ tsp.
- Freshly ground black pepper - ¼ tsp.

Procedure:

1. Using a large saucepan, add in oil and heat. Mix in garlic and sauté until browned lightly for about 1 minute, ensure it doesn't burn. Mix in the basil and tomatoes. Add in pepper and salt for seasoning. Cook for 10 minutes over medium heat while uncovered.
2. Serve over pasta, grains, beans, or vegetables.

Nutrition per serving:

Calories: 103, Total Fat: 5g, Saturated Fat: 1g, Cholesterol: 0mg, Sodium: 32mg, Potassium: 735mg, Total Carbs: 15g, Fiber: 3g, Sugars: 0g, Protein: 3g

13.9 Greek Yogurt Dressing with Basil

Serves: 2 cups | Preparation Time: 5 minutes | Cooking Time: 10 minutes

Ingredients:

- chopped fresh basil - ¼ c.
- chopped sage - ¼ c.
- nonfat (0%) plain Greek yogurt - 1 c. (240mL)
- chopped fresh coriander - ½ c.
- minced onion - 1
- minced cloves garlic - 2
- extra-virgin olive oil - 2 tbsps.
- juice from 1 orange - 2 tbsps.
- maple syrup - ½ tsp.
- salt - ⅛ tsp.
- ground black pepper - ⅛ tsp.

Procedure:

1. Mix together the basil, coriander, and sage in your food processor and puree a few times until they have been ground up slightly. Scrape down the sides.
2. Pour in the onion, garlic, Greek yogurt, olive oil, salt, orange juice, ¼ cup water, maple syrup, and pepper and puree until smooth and ingredients have been fully incorporated.
3. Enjoy or refrigerate for a maximum of 1 week.

Nutrition per serving:

Calories: 26, Total fat: 2 g, Saturated fat: <1 g, Total carbs: 1 g, Protein: 2 g, Cholesterol: <1 mg, Sodium: 27 mg, Potassium: 53 mg, Fiber: <1 g, Sugars: 1 g

13.10 Meaty Spaghetti Sauce

Serves: 6 | Preparation Time: 15 minutes | Cooking Time: 30 minutes

Ingredients:

- ground 95% lean beef, extra-lean - 1 pound
- no salt added tomato sauce - 1 (15 oz.) can
- no salt added diced tomatoes - 1 (14½ oz.) can
- garlic cloves, minced or squeezed through garlic press - 2
- chopped onions (fresh or frozen) - ½ c.
- Italian seasoning - 1 tsp.
- dried basil - 1 tsp.

Procedure:

1. In a nonstick skillet set over a medium high source of heat, mix in ground beef and cook for 3 minutes. Turn down heat to medium intensity. Add in garlic and onions. Proceed with the cooking for 5 additional minutes, or until browned well.
2. Add diced tomatoes and tomato sauce and simmer 10 - 15 minutes. Sprinkle seasonings in last few minutes of cooking.

Nutrition per serving:

Calories: 184, Protein: 23 g, Carbs: 8 g, Fat: 7 g, Cholesterol: 67 mg, Fiber: 2 g, Sodium: 105 mg, Potassium: 733 mg

13.11 Creamy Avocado Cilantro Lime Dressing

Serves: 2 | Preparation Time: 5 minutes | Cooking Time: 0 minutes

Ingredients:

- diced avocado - 1
- water - ½ c.
- cilantro leaves - ¼ c.
- fresh lime or lemon juice (about 2 limes or lemons) - ¼ c.
- ground cumin - ½ tsp.

Procedure:

1. Using a blender, add all the ingredients (high-speed blenders work best for this), and pulse until well combined. Add more seasoning if need be. It is best served within 1 day.

Nutrition per serving:

Calories: 94, Fat: 7.4g, Carbs: 5.7g, Protein: 1.1g, Fiber: 3.5g, Sodium: 67mg, Potassium 176mg.

13.12 Maple Dijon Dressing

Serves: 1 | Preparation Time: 5 minutes | Cooking Time: 0 minutes

Ingredients:

- apple cider vinegar - ¼ c.
- Dijon mustard - 2 tsps.
- maple syrup - 2 tbsps.
- low-sodium vegetable broth - 2 tbsps.
- black pepper - ¼ tsp.

Procedure:

1. Using a resealable container, mix the apple cider vinegar, maple syrup, vegetable broth, Dijon mustard, and black pepper until well incorporated.
2. The dressing can be refrigerated for a maximum of 5 days.

Nutrition per serving:

Calories: 82, Fat: 0.3g, Carbs: 19.3g, Protein: 0.6g, Fiber: 0.7g, Sodium: 53mg, Potassium: 67mg.

13.13 Tahini Lemon Dressing

Serves: makes ½ cup | Preparation Time: 5 minutes | Cooking Time: 0

Ingredients:

- pure maple syrup - ¼ tsp.
- tahini - ¼ c.
- warm water - 3 tbsps.
- cumin (ground) - ¼ tsp.
- kosher salt - ¼ tsp.
- lemon juice - 3 tbsps.
- cayenne pepper - ⅛ tsp.

Procedure:

1. Using a bowl, add in water, cumin, salt, cayenne pepper, tahini, lemon juice, and maple syrup. Mix well to make the mixture smooth.
2. Place in the refrigerator until ready to serve.
3. Store any leftovers in an airtight container and place in your refrigerator for a maximum of 5 days.

Nutrition per serving:

Calories: 91, Total fat: 7.3g, Saturated fat: 1.1g, Cholesterol: 0mg, Sodium: 80mg, Potassium: 77mg, Total Carbs:

5g, Fiber: 1g, Sugars: 1g, Protein: 3g, Magnesium: 15mg, Calcium: 66mg

13.14 Tahini Yogurt Dressing

Serves: makes 1 cup | Preparation Time: 5 minutes | Cooking Time: 0

Ingredients:

- plain Greek yogurt - ½ c.
- tahini - ⅓ c.
- freshly squeezed orange juice - ¼ c.
- kosher salt - ½ tsp.

Procedure:

1. Using a mixing bowl, add in tahini, orange juice and salt. Mix well until the tahini becomes smooth. Add more juice if needed to help smooth it out.
2. Refrigerate until when ready to serve.
3. Store any leftovers in an airtight container and place in the refrigerator for a maximum of 5 days.

Nutrition per serving:

Calories: 70, Total fat: 2.1g, Saturated fat: 1.1g, Cholesterol: 0mg, Sodium: 80mg, Potassium: 85mg, Total Carbs: 4g, Fiber: 1.1g, Sugars: 1g, Protein: 4.2g, Magnesium: 12mg, Calcium: 66mg

14 10 WEEKS MEAL PLAN

Week 1

Day	Breakfast/Smoothie	Lunch	Dinner	Dessert/ Snack/ Side
Monday	Millet Cream	Cilantro Halibut	Black-Bean and Vegetable Burrito	Walnut Cake
Tuesday	Blueberry-Vanilla Yogurt Smoothie	Roasted Brussels Sprouts	Turkey with Spring Onions	Strawberries and Coconut Bowls
Wednesday	Refreshing Mango and Pear Smoothie	Pasta with Peas & Tomatoes	Pork with Cherry Tomatoes	Corn and Cayenne Pepper Spread
Thursday	Sausage Casserole	Parsnip and Turkey Bites	Ginger Sea Bass	Hot Walnuts
Friday	Bean Casserole	White Beans with Spinach and Pan-Roasted Tomatoes	Garam Masala Turkey	Coconut and Cinnamon Cream
Saturday	Tropical Green Breakfast Smoothie	Cod and Asparagus	Basil Turkey	Nuts And Seeds Mix
Sunday	Cheese Hash Browns	Spiced Meat with Endives	Veggies Stuffed Bell Peppers	Grapefruit Compote

Week 2

Day	Breakfast/Smoothie	Lunch	Dinner	Dessert/ Snack/ Side
Monday	Tropical Turmeric Smoothie	Roasted Kabocha with Wild Rice	Five-Spices Sole	Cocoa Squares
Tuesday	The Amazing Feta Hash	Veggie Pita Rolls	Cilantro Beef Meatballs	Radish Chips
Wednesday	Artichoke Eggs	Chicken with Tomatoes and Celery Stalk	Butternut-Squash Macaroni and Cheese	Soy Sauce Green Beans
Thursday	Banana Breakfast Smoothie	Shallot and Salmon Mix	Cheddar Turkey	Rice and Fruits Pudding
Friday	Apples and Raisins Bowls	Nutmeg Chicken with Tender Chickpeas	Vegetarian Black Bean Pasta	Black Beans Bars
Saturday	Raspberry Green Smoothie	Couscous with Beans & Vegetables	Greek Flatbread with Spinach, Tomatoes & Feta	Kale Chips
Sunday	Scallions and Sesame Seeds Omelet	Cilantro Beef Meatballs	Zucchini Black Bean Tacos	Coconut Shred Bars

Week 3

Day	Breakfast/Smoothie	Lunch	Dinner	Dessert/ Snack/ Side
Monday	Tomato and Spinach Eggs	Chicken with Tomatoes	Easy Beet and Goat Cheese Risotto	Nutritious Snack Bowls
Tuesday	Chocolate and Peanut Butter Smoothie	Limes and Shrimps Skewers	Spiced Meat with Endives	Cinnamon Plums
Wednesday	Dill Omelet	Meat and Zucchini Mix	Lentil Medley	Spiced Walnuts
Thursday	Carrot Juice Smoothie	Veggies Stuffed Bell Peppers	Chicken Bowl with Red Cabbage	Carrot Chips
Friday	Omelet with Peppers	Huevos Rancheros	Beef with Cauliflower Rice	Lime Cake
Saturday	Ultimate Fruit Smoothie	Curried Cauliflower with Chickpeas	Tender Salmon with Chives	Sour Cream Green Beans
Sunday	Sausage Casserole	Zucchini Black Bean Tacos	Spiced Meat with Endives	Pepper and Chickpeas Hummus

Week 4

Day	Breakfast/Smoothie	Lunch	Dinner	Dessert/ Snack/ Side
Monday	Peaches And Greens Smoothie	Minty Avocado Soup	Spinach Soufflés	Rhubarb and Pear Compote
Tuesday	Artichoke Eggs	Black-Bean and Vegetable Burrito	Garlic Turkey	Vanilla Apple Cake
Wednesday	Millet Cream	Warm Spiced Cabbage Bake	Baked Sweet Potatoes with Cumin	Minty Tapenade
Thursday	Blueberry Smoothie	Butternut-Squash Macaroni and Cheese	Roasted Kabocha with Wild Rice	Cumin Brussels Sprouts
Friday	Oat Cocoa Smoothie	Tuna and Pineapple Kebob	Chicken Sandwich	Baked Apples with Nuts
Saturday	Cheese Hash Browns	Mushroom and Eggplant Casserole	Garlic Pork	Hearty Buttery Walnuts
Sunday	Raspberry Green Smoothie	Zucchini with Corn	Parsley Shrimp	Lemony Chickpeas Dip

Week 5

Day	Breakfast/Smoothie	Lunch	Dinner	Dessert/ Snack/ Side
Monday	Strawberry Sandwich	Coconut Avocado Soup	Fennel and Salmon	Instant Pot Applesauce
Tuesday	Chocolate Berry Smoothie	Turkey and Zucchini Tortillas	Black-Eyed Peas and Greens Power Salad	Red Pepper Muffins with Mozzarella
Wednesday	The Amazing Feta Hash	Coconut Cod	Chicken with Tomatoes	Tortilla Chips with Chili
Thursday	Satisfying Berry and Almond Smoothie	Garam Masala Turkey	Roasted Brussels Sprouts	Hot Walnuts
Friday	Blackberry and Apple Smoothie	Cast Iron Roots and Grain	Curried Cauliflower with Chickpeas	Green Tea and Banana Sweetening Mix
Saturday	Tomato and Spinach Eggs	Lentil Medley	Baked Cod	Minty Tapenade
Sunday	Green Apple Smoothie	Basil Turkey	Rosemary Endives	Nutritious Snack Bowls

Week 6

Day	Breakfast/Smoothie	Lunch	Dinner	Dessert/ Snack/ Side
Monday	Mixed Berries Smoothie	Chunky Black-Bean Dip	Paprika Chicken	Nuts And Seeds Mix
Tuesday	Avocado Smoothie	Easy Chickpea Veggie Burgers	Chicken with Eggplants	Cranberry Crackers
Wednesday	Scallions and Sesame Seeds Omelet	Mushroom Barley Soup	Limes and Shrimps Skewers	Grapefruit Compote
Thursday	Blueberry-Vanilla Yogurt Smoothie	Vegetarian Black Bean Pasta	Hot Chicken Mix	Carrot Chips
Friday	Apples and Raisins Bowls	Cheddar Turkey	Healthy Vegetable Fried Rice	Pepper and Chickpeas Hummus
Saturday	Tropical Green Breakfast Smoothie	Ginger Sea Bass	Cilantro Beef Meatballs	Potato Chips
Sunday	Bean Casserole	Pork with Cherry Tomatoes	Red Beans and Rice	Cinnamon Plums

Week 7

Day	Breakfast/Smoothie	Lunch	Dinner	Dessert/ Snack/ Side
Monday	Dill Omelet	Acorn Squash & Coconut Creamed Greens Casserole	White Beans with Spinach and Pan-Roasted Tomatoes	Walnut Cake
Tuesday	Blackberry and Apple Smoothie	Chicken Bowl with Red Cabbage	Zucchini with Corn	Corn and Cayenne Pepper Spread
Wednesday	Omelet with Peppers	Paprika Chicken	Pasta with Peas & Tomatoes	Instant Pot Applesauce
Thursday	Oat Cocoa Smoothie	Baked Cod	Polenta Squares with Cheese & Pine Nuts	Peach And Carrots
Friday	Tropical Turmeric Smoothie	Eggplant Parmesan	Couscous with Beans & Vegetables	Cocoa Squares
Saturday	Refreshing Mango and Pear Smoothie	Spiced Meat with Endives	Cilantro Halibut	Tortilla Chips with Chili
Sunday	Scallions and Sesame Seeds Omelet	Baked Sweet Potatoes with Cumin	Thyme Pork Skillet	Coconut and Cinnamon Cream

Week 8

Day	Breakfast/Smoothie	Lunch	Dinner	Dessert/ Snack/ Side
Monday	Banana Breakfast Smoothie	Mustard and Garlic Chicken	Huevos Rancheros	Green Tea and Banana Sweetening Mix
Tuesday	Green Apple Smoothie	Fennel and Salmon	Warm Spiced Cabbage Bake	Aromatic Avocado Fries
Wednesday	Sausage Casserole	Celery, Cucumber and Zucchini Soup	Veggie Pita Rolls	Kale Chips
Thursday	Mixed Berries Smoothie	Turkey with Spring Onions	Easy Chickpea Veggie Burgers	Spiced Broccoli Florets
Friday	Artichoke Eggs	Easy Beet and Goat Cheese Risotto	Parsnip and Turkey Bites	Red Pepper Muffins with Mozzarella
Saturday	Blueberry Smoothie	Hot Chicken Mix	Coconut Cod	Radish Chips
Sunday	Cheese Hash Browns	Five-Spices Sole	Turkey and Zucchini Tortillas	Rice and Fruits Pudding

Week 9

Day	Breakfast/Smoothie	Lunch	Dinner	Dessert/ Snack/ Side
Monday	Chocolate Berry Smoothie	Garlic Pork	Tuna and Pineapple Kebob	Carrot Sticks with Onion and Sour Cream
Tuesday	Ultimate Fruit Smoothie	Spinach Soufflés	Cilantro Beef Meatballs	Baked Apples with Nuts
Wednesday	Dill Omelet	Parsley Shrimp	Cast Iron Roots and Grain	Coconut Shred Bars
Thursday	Avocado Smoothie	Chicken with Eggplants	Eggplant Parmesan	Lemony Chickpeas Dip
Friday	Omelet with Peppers	Red Beans and Rice	Nutmeg Chicken with Tender Chickpeas	Potato Chips
Saturday	Satisfying Berry and Almond Smoothie	Thyme Pork Skillet	Cod and Asparagus	Rhubarb and Pear Compote
Sunday	Millet Cream	Rosemary Endives	Chicken Sandwich	Hearty Buttery Walnuts

Week 10

Day	Breakfast/Smoothie	Lunch	Dinner	Dessert/ Snack/ Side
Monday	The Amazing Feta Hash	Tender Salmon with Chives	Acorn Squash & Coconut Creamed Greens Casserole	Vanilla Apple Cake
Tuesday	Peaches And Greens Smoothie	Polenta Squares with Cheese & Pine Nuts	Shallot and Salmon Mix	Cranberry Crackers
Wednesday	Chocolate and Peanut Butter Smoothie	Beef with Cauliflower Rice	Mushroom and Eggplant Casserole	Strawberries and Coconut Bowls
Thursday	Tomato and Spinach Eggs	Black-Eyed Peas and Greens Power Salad	Mustard and Garlic Chicken	Aromatic Avocado Fries
Friday	Strawberry Sandwich	Garlic Turkey	Chunky Black-Bean Dip	Spiced Walnuts
Saturday	Carrot Juice Smoothie	Healthy Vegetable Fried Rice	Meat and Zucchini Mix	Black Beans Bars
Sunday	Apples and Raisins Bowls	Greek Flatbread with Spinach, Tomatoes & Feta	Chicken with Tomatoes and Celery Stalk	Lime Cake

15 MEASUREMENTS

Volume Equivalents (Dry)	
US STANDARD	METRIC (APPROXIMATE)
1/8 teaspoon	0.5 mL
1/4 teaspoon	1 mL
1/2 teaspoon	2 mL
3/4 teaspoon	4 mL
1 teaspoon	5 mL
1 tablespoon	15 mL
1/4 cup	59 mL
1/2 cup	118 mL
3/4 cup	177 mL
1 cup	235 mL
2 cups	475 mL
3 cups	700 mL
4 cups	1 L

Temperature Equivalents	
FAHRENHEIT (F)	METRIC (APPROXIMATE)
225 °F	107 °C
250 °F	120 °C
275 °F	135 °C
300 °F	150 °C
325 °F	160 °C
350 °F	180 °C
375 °F	190 °C
400 °F	205 °C
425 °F	220 °C
450 °F	235 °C
475 °F	245 °C
500 °F	260 °C

Volume Equivalents (Liquid)		
US STANDARD	US STANDARD (OUNCES)	METRIC (APPROX.)
2 tablespoons	1 fl. oz.	30 mL
1/4 cup	2 fl. oz.	60 mL
1/2 cup	4 fl. oz.	120 mL
1 cup	8 fl. oz.	240 mL
1 1/2 cup	12 fl. oz.	355 mL
2 cups or 1 pint	16 fl. oz.	475 mL
4 cups or 1 quart	32 fl. oz.	1 L
1 gallon	128 fl. oz.	4 L

Weight Equivalents	
US STANDARD	METRIC (APPROXIMATE)
1 ounce	28 g
2 ounces	57 g
5 ounces	142 g
10 ounces	284 g
15 ounces	425 g
16 ounces (1 pound)	455 g
1.5 pounds	680 g
2 pounds	907 g

16 CONCLUSION

Dash diet is an excellent choice for individuals who aspire to shed some weight and improve their wellness or health. It's also a diet plan you can follow without thinking of its side effects. If you're overweight or obese, then this diet will assist you in losing weight effectively, naturally, and simply because it focuses on whole foods that are rich in nutrients, unlike other diets, which include processed foods with artificial chemicals. The Dash diet program is an excellent approach to improving your overall health and quality of life through simple eating habits.

BONUS: Scanning the following QR code will take you to a web page where you can access 7 fantastic bonuses after leaving your email and an honest review of my book on Amazon: five online courses about sushi making and 2 mobile apps with other sushi recipes.

Link: https://dl.bookfunnel.com/3vb7s6tbdw

Printed in Great Britain
by Amazon